IGNITE *the* LIGHT

Also by Vicki Savini

THE LIGHT INSIDE OF ME

❊

Hay House Titles of Related Interest

THE ASTONISHING POWER OF EMOTIONS: Let Your Feelings Be Your Guide, by Esther and Jerry Hicks (The Teachings of Abraham™)

EXCUSES BEGONE! How to Change Lifelong, Self-Defeating Thinking Habits, by Dr. Wayne W. Dyer

THE INDIGO CHILDREN: The New Kids Have Arrived, by Lee Carroll and Jan Tober

THE INTUITIVE SPARK: Bringing Intuition Home to Your Child, Your Family, and You, by Sonia Choquette

WHO WOULD YOU BE WITHOUT YOUR STORY? Dialogues with Byron Katie, edited by Carol Williams

Please visit:

Hay House USA: www.hayhouse.com®
Hay House Australia: www.hayhouse.com.au
Hay House UK: www.hayhouse.co.uk
Hay House South Africa: www.hayhouse.co.za
Hay House India: www.hayhouse.co.in

IGNITE *the* LIGHT

EMPOWERING CHILDREN AND ADULTS TO BE THEIR ABSOLUTE BEST

VICKI SAVINI

HAY HOUSE, INC.
Carlsbad, California • New York City
London • Sydney • Johannesburg
Vancouver • Hong Kong • New Delhi

Copyright © 2014 by Vicki Savini

Published and distributed in the United States by: Hay House, Inc.: www.hay house.com® • *Published and distributed in Australia by:* Hay House Australia Pty. Ltd.: www.hayhouse.com.au • *Published and distributed in the United Kingdom by:* Hay House UK, Ltd.: www.hayhouse.co.uk • *Published and distributed in the Republic of South Africa by:* Hay House SA (Pty), Ltd.: www.hayhouse.co.za • *Distributed in Canada by:* Raincoast Books: www.raincoast.com • *Published in India by:* Hay House Publishers India: www.hayhouse.co.in

Cover design: Mary Ann Smith • *Interior design:* Tricia Breidenthal
Interior illustrations: Vicki Savini

Cataloging-in-Publication Data is on file with the Library of Congress

Tradepaper ISBN: 978-1-4019-4326-4

17 16 15 14   4 3 2 1
1st edition, May 2014

Printed in the United States of America

I dedicate this book to the children who walk the earth today, the children who dwell deep within our hearts, and the children who have yet to come. May you shine brighter than our most brilliant stars in the sky, and may you find comfort in your own skin—

today, tomorrow, and always.

CONTENTS

AUTHOR'S NOTE

When I sat down a few years ago to write this book, I really had no idea what was coming out of me and where this was headed. All I knew was that I had to get my thoughts onto paper because it felt right in every fiber of my being. I honestly cannot take full credit for some of the material because it doesn't necessarily come directly *from* me. Often, when I write, I am awakened and inspired in the middle of the night with thoughts and ideas to teach important lessons. I would therefore say that some of the information provided in this book has come *through* me. This has been happening for a good 20 years now, but I've finally realized that my part in all of this is to simply get out of my own way and allow the lessons to flow freely. This is one way I honor the light within myself.

I believe that we are all here for a purpose and that we know somewhere deep inside our hearts what that purpose is, yet it takes time and life experience as the years go by and our lives unfold to remember who we truly are. It is when we have learned to *feel* our feelings, love ourselves, and speak our truth that the light within shines bright and we are guided to our higher purpose. It is my hope that from reading this book, something will spark inside of you and you will not only ignite the light within, but more important, you will ignite the light *within our children*. I am on a journey of life just like you, and I feel truly honored that our paths have crossed.

So, who am I? I am a teacher who has taught elementary education in public schools for the past 15 years of my life. I'm not a typical teacher because I've crossed the conventional lines of education by inviting yoga, meditation, mirror work, energy healing, and affirmations into my public school classroom. I have a distinctive understanding of childhood because I *see the world through the eyes of a child.* I am honored to have this gift and take it as a compliment when I am reminded of it, because seeing the world this way gives me the remarkable ability to bring out the very best in the children I work with. I am also a life coach who uses my eclectic training in Reiki, Science of Mind, and intuition to inspire adults to look deep within in order to discover negative core beliefs that began in childhood and currently cause havoc or hold them back in life.

For years, I have worked with children and adults separately and wondered what the connection was and how I could possibly marry the two. Recently, that answer was revealed to me. I noticed that when I work with children, I am giving them tools to use today and in the future to be their absolute best—creating a strong foundation. And when I work with adults, I have found that I am giving them those same tools to *repair and strengthen* the foundation they were given in childhood.

A few years ago I wrote a children's book titled *The Light Inside of Me* to help children make good choices by aligning with what *feels* right. I created this book because I believe that we all have "light" inside of us—a place deep in our hearts that shines brightly when we are in the flow of life and dims when we are driven by fear. Some would call this our higher self or God self. I simply call it the light within.

For years I have gone through life with the mind-set that childhood is too precious to ignore. I firmly believe this because we are creating thoughts for our children, which then turn into *their* beliefs during this time period. Too often, these thoughts are based on our own core beliefs that are currently creating some sort of havoc in *our* lives. If we want to bring the very best out in our children, then we need to give them *essential tools* during their childhood so that they can navigate the waters of life more successfully in adulthood. If we want our children to shine, then we must ignite the light within.

I am a teacher, a mother, a wife, a life coach, and the list goes on, but when I strip the titles away and look at my inner being, I am a woman on a mission. My mission is to educate, enlighten, and empower as many children and adults as possible by replacing negative core beliefs with positive core beliefs so that everyone can be their absolute best and simply shine. From my experience working with both children and adults, I can honestly say that if we can give children positive core beliefs and tools to uphold those beliefs later in life, then our adult struggles will decrease immensely. On the flip side, if we don't take the time to pinpoint the beliefs that are holding *us* back, and we just keep moving forward without this valuable knowledge, then we ultimately pass on these negative beliefs to our children or the children we serve.

INTRODUCTION

Just Imagine

Have you ever stopped to think about the importance of childhood? We all had a childhood experience, and it was a critical time period in our lives because most of our beliefs were shaped there and many of our tools for life were formed there. The true question is, were we given the tools we truly need to be our absolute best—to ignite the light within?

Imagine a world where children go to school and are not only given books, pencils, and computers as tools for learning, but more important, they are given tools for life that help them to be the best possible version of themselves. Just for a moment, envision a place where children learn very early on how to manifest their hearts' desires by learning how to tap into the true self that is deep within. Every day, children would be taught to honor the light within and to love themselves unconditionally. They would be allowed to *feel* their feelings and recognize those feelings as an important gauge for decision making. All children would learn techniques to quiet the noise around them, especially the noise within their own minds. Listening would take on a whole new meaning as children learned how to listen to the voice within and be mindful and considerate of the feelings and opinions of others. In a world where so much negativity exists, wouldn't it be amazing if children were taught how to turn toxic thoughts into positive ones? How wonderful it would be if kids understood the power of their thoughts and realized that these thoughts become beliefs that ultimately become reality. These lessons would empower children to speak their truth even if their voices felt a bit shaky. Imagine an education system focused on the power of community rather than competition. Imagine a world where children are taught that we are not separate, but instead, we are all a part of something much bigger than ourselves—we are one.

I imagined this world many years ago while I was studying to be a teacher. Then and there I promised myself that I would make a positive impact in the lives of children. I truly believe that childhood is too precious to ignore. Childhood is our foundation. It is the ground floor from which we set our life's journey in motion. It's impossible to believe that *what happens in childhood stays in childhood,* because these early experiences remain with us and affect us all the days of our lives.

Some children are lucky enough to have amazing foundations driven completely by love. These children are nurtured, loved, and taught to believe in themselves and remember who they truly are from a very young age. Others are taught lessons of both love and fear. These children have some foundations in love that give them the ability to positively move forward in life, but may also have some fear-driven beliefs that cause them to question their own abilities or hold themselves back from achieving their bliss later in life. A third group is made up of those whose foundations are more unstable and rooted primarily in fear. These children grow up in an environment that is insecure and more difficult to thrive in.

Most people can relate to one of these three categories, both in thinking about their own childhood or that of their children. Because of the major impact the early years have on the rest of a person's life, I believe it is not only imperative that we build strong foundations, but also critical to examine our own foundations and take the time to make repairs where needed.

Through this book, I hope that you will embrace the opportunity to rethink how you view and treat children *during* childhood. No matter if you are a parent, a teacher, or a person looking to leave the world a little better than you found it, I am optimistic that you will be able to see how your own childhood impacted your life as you know it today. I believe we are in a time of great change—education, parenting, and the world are all changing. In this change lies great opportunity. But this is also a time of great turmoil. Just watch the news or open a newspaper and you'll see how challenging and scary the world can be for young people:

- It is estimated that 160,000 children miss school every day due to fear of attack or intimidation by other students. (*Source:* National Education Association)

- One in seven students in grades K to 12 is either a bully or a victim of bullying. (*Source:* Dan Olweus, National School Safety Center)

- Depressive disorders affect approximately 18.8 million American adults or about 9.5 percent of the U.S. population ages 18 and older in a given year. (*Source:* NIMH, Science on Our Minds Fact Sheet)

In writing this book, I hope to encourage parents and educators to look at childhood from a different perspective. Please don't think of this as a parenting book or an educator's text. Instead, consider it a message of hope, a manual for change. *Ignite the Light* offers simple and practical solutions to some of society's most pressing issues, including bullying and depression.

Using This Book

This book is intended to help you recognize how core beliefs affect us daily, realize the alternatives to negative beliefs, and respond by taking action to shift those beliefs and ignite the light within. I write about my experiences with children and adults and give you tools that you can immediately apply in the classroom, at home, or in your daily life.

In the first section, See the Light, I set out to heighten your awareness of childhood and core beliefs. You will be awakened by reading about the importance of childhood and a theory that sets the stage for explaining how we got to where we are today. You will be able to get a different perspective by seeing the world through the eyes of a child as I do and perhaps understanding the child within. You will be gently guided to discover the core beliefs that are holding you back in life and preventing you from creating strong foundations for yourself and the children you affect on a daily basis. In this section you will also be able to identify key behaviors and habits that lead to a strong foundation based in love, acceptance, and understanding.

In Part II, Ignite the Light, I will introduce the seven essentials that will not only help you *create* strong foundations for children, but also repair and strengthen your own foundation so that you can be the best possible version of yourself. This section of the book discusses the alternatives that will help you to teach children how to *respond* to life, instead of *reacting* to it. In the long run, it all comes back to our foundation. If we want to make positive changes for our children, we must first take a look in the mirror and be willing to ignite the light within.

Finally, Part III, Be the Light, is your toolbox to put the seven essentials into immediate practice so that *you* can educate, enlighten, and empower yourself and the children you serve. You will be given practical tools to apply to children in the classroom, in your home, and to your very own inner child. Whether you are a parent, an educator, or a concerned individual, you will be able to help children build strong foundations at an early age that will ultimately empower them to be their personal best. If we truly want to see a positive change in the world, we need to start with ourselves. If we honestly believe that the children *are* the future, we need to invest time and energy in ourselves so that we can be *our* personal best, and then teach our children to be *their* personal best.

Igniting the Light . . . Together

I am who I am because I'm a problem solver. As I've said, I see the world through the eyes of a child, and I embrace their inner light with my heart and soul. That has made me an effective teacher not only academically, but (and this is more important) emotionally. I love getting notes from high school seniors who remember my classroom not necessarily because of something academic that I taught, but because of how they *felt* there. My kids learn how to problem solve, stand up for themselves and others, believe in themselves, and speak their truth effectively. They feel empowered and that's why they're at their personal best—academically, socially, and emotionally.

I strongly believe that everything that happens during childhood impacts who we become as adults. As a teacher and a mother, I strive to teach my children to believe in themselves and speak their truth from a very young age. I want each of them to have the ability to look in the mirror and know and love the person staring back at them. It is my greatest hope that someday all children will be able to look in the mirror and see a beautiful reflection of love and acceptance.

I've realized in the past few years, though, that by being in the classroom I am limited in how many kids I can affect. This is where I need your help. My goal is to change the face of education, but I'm realizing that I can't do it alone. I know that there are more teachers, child-care providers, and parents out there just like me, who maybe just need a little push to step outside of the box or a reminder that it's okay—and more important, very necessary—to give this gift to our children.

Won't you please join me on this journey of changing the face of education and empowering our children to be their absolute best today so that tomorrow won't have to be such a struggle? If we all contribute to this movement by making small adjustments, we'll ultimately create huge changes for our children. I'm tired of hearing about bullying and violence in our schools. Martin Luther King, Jr., once said, "Hate cannot drive out hate; only love can do that." The only remedy to fear is love, and by teaching our children simple strategies at a young age, we can diminish the violence greatly and bring out the very best in *all* of our children.

I know in my heart that the only way to make this happen is to educate, enlighten, and empower the adults who guide children in this life. Just imagine all of the problems we could solve if each of us took the time to repair and strengthen our own foundation and then helped our children access these self-care tools at a much younger age.

Get your toolbox for life out of the closet and brace yourself for an amazing journey. I am a woman on a mission who knows that it only takes one spark to ignite the light. I can't wait to see the extreme brightness that floods the Universe when *you* ignite the light within yourself and the children around you!

PART I

SEE
THE
LIGHT

A BRIEF MOMENT IN TIME

"Childhood is a short season."

— HELEN HAYES

Early one cold November morning, I walked into a local coffee shop and said hello to some of the regulars. As I waited in line to order my yummy mocha latte, I noticed a toddler with his dad. He was a jovial child with an inquisitive look in his eyes. His father sat him in a wooden high chair and stood close by to give the barista his order. I noticed that the sun was shining in the little boy's face, yet he was mesmerized by the design on the chair and appeared unaffected by the brightness. His hands gently caressed this newfound object, and his eyes were intense with wonder. I caught myself in the moment, staring at this beautiful child in the sunlight, and then glanced around. I smiled when I noticed that the majority of the people in the coffee shop were doing exactly what I was doing: marveling at this little boy who was basking in the sun and filling himself with the wonder of life. It was as if time stopped for a moment and we were all connected as we watched this young child simply *be*.

Why is it that no matter where you go, or how many people are present, when you see a child laughing, giggling, or exploring their world with joy, you can't help but turn and look? The instant your eyes settle on the child enjoying the moment, you feel a sense of calm and comfort. You're taken back to your innocence, to a time when things were simple and new. It is moments like these that take us beyond our thoughts and connect us to something buried deep within.

Childhood: A Dwindling Era

Childhood is a brief time period that begins at birth and ends at puberty. Considering that the average life span is about 80 years, some might conclude that childhood, which lasts about 13 years, is insignificant in the grand scheme of things. After all, it's short and occurs very early on. However, the truth is that *childhood is the most critical time period of our entire lives* because it sets the stage for our journey into adulthood.

Intellectually, we know just how brief childhood is when viewing it in the context of an entire lifetime, but how *mindful* of this short time period are we? It seems that we rush our children through their days and try to turn them into miniature adults as soon as possible. As a parent and a teacher, I have come to realize that oftentimes we aren't even cognizant of how our actions affect our children. In our fast-paced society, adults expect young children to sit and listen for long periods of time. This has led to the elimination of play breaks in elementary school and the overprogramming of students both in school and through extracurricular activities during their "free" time. Today's students are constantly on the go, pressured to learn more, do more, achieve more, and be more. And at the end of grade school we heap more stress on these kids, reminding them just how difficult middle school will be and how important it is for them to "get it together" by the end of the year. This continues as they transition into high school as well. It's difficult for these children to quiet their minds, because they never have true downtime.

Perhaps this busyness is just a reflection of adult life in our society, because it's very common for children to see their parents running from one activity or commitment to the next, not taking time to quiet their own minds. The media also contributes to the untimely rush into adulthood, as it becomes more and more difficult to shield our children from news of shootings, wars, and overall violence sweeping the planet.

As clichéd as it sounds, I do believe that the children are our future. More important, I believe that our childhood determines how smooth or difficult our journey through adulthood will be. Everyone talks about the need to make changes in our schools and in society to bring out the best in our children, yet actions speak louder than words, and it's safe to say that it's time for action.

Life experience has taught me that you can't solve a problem when you are simply reacting to that problem. As Albert Einstein said, no problem can be solved from the same level of the consciousness that created it. When your focus is on the issue at hand, you are unable to see the light in the darkness. You have a tendency to react to life instead of responding to it, and your mind becomes cluttered with fearful thoughts. Therefore, you can't truly solve a problem until you are aware of its roots. I believe that these roots take hold in childhood. Therefore, the first step in bringing out the very best in our children is *awareness*.

If we want to bring out the very best in our children, then we need to take a look at the foundations we are laying for them during childhood. We must ask ourselves if we are giving our children the tools they need to navigate life successfully and find their own truth. From this strong foundation they will learn to believe in themselves and above all, speak their truth, even when their voices shake.

When the School Bell Rings

In American schools, we currently spend our time "racing to the top," yet we say we want "no child left behind." I invite you to read that sentence again and take a close look at the words. When was the last time you watched a *race* in which someone was *not left behind*?

Now, let me say that this next section of the book contains material that is specific to the American education system and which you may or may not be familiar with. This section is certainly more cerebral than the following pages. However, I encourage you to read through it to gain an understanding of how our current education system will affect our children in the future by adding unnecessary pressures to their childhood today. I assure you that it is brief but necessary information to heighten your awareness of issues that our children are currently contending with.

In the American education system we have two seemingly contradictory government initiatives that started out as intentions to help children but ultimately have created a great deal of stress and anxiety.

The United States Congress set into motion education reform that was built on the belief that setting high standards and establishing measurable goals through standardized testing would improve individual outcomes in education. This was the No Child Left Behind Act (NCLB) of 2001. The act required all states to establish assessments (or tests) focusing on basic skills and provide these assessments to all students at a specific grade level in order to receive federal school funding. Standards were set by each state individually, but NCLB expanded the federal role in public education through annual testing, annual academic progress tracking, report cards, teacher qualifications standards, and funding changes.

Race to the Top is a United States Department of Education contest aimed at "closing the education achievement gap" and spurring innovation and reform in the country's poorest school districts. States are awarded points for satisfying certain educational policies including performance-based standards (often referred to as an annual professional performance review or APPR) for teachers and principals, complying with nationwide standards, promoting charter schools and privatization of education, and computerization. Grants are available to those who qualify.

Both of these education reform acts (No Child Left Behind, signed into law in 2001, and Race to the Top, passed in 2009) originated with good intent, but they have led to unfair practices and pressures in our classrooms that contribute to the disintegration of childhood. Through the push to close the gap and increase test scores, we have lost sight of the importance of childhood—of the need for children to play, grow, and learn at their own pace.

Today, teachers are constantly asked to prove the effectiveness of their teaching and are not necessarily trusted to make decisions as to what's best for their own students. They're currently being instructed to spend significant amounts of time documenting their instruction in order to prove it works, while students are given more rigorous tests to show standardized growth. Students are being tested at the beginning of the school year in areas they can't possibly do well in, only to ensure they will "improve" throughout the year and measure a certain percentage of growth. Teachers are required to track this "growth" in order to be deemed successful and keep their jobs.

The sad truth, in my opinion, is that not much of this testing enhances the student. Instead, all of this data collection puts unnecessary pressure on the teachers and students to compete for government funding to provide *necessary* school resources. The primary issue with all of this is that our children are not necessarily getting the education that they deserve because there is too much time spent on documentation and testing and not enough time connecting with our kids and teaching them how to believe in themselves. There is something unique and amazing about every child, and standardization hides their innate splendor.

Stress levels are high and morale is low for both the students and faculty when fear is leading the way. Students quickly become numbers when data collection takes precedence over educating the whole child. With all of this data collection, testing, and pressure, there is little time for kids to just be kids and enjoy the learning process. In trying to improve our education system, somehow we've managed to damage it further. The clear message many children are getting from all of this is that they're just not good enough. In my experience, the result of all of this pressure is an increase in everything we don't want: bullying, depression, anxiety, and stress.

Distinguished teachers take the time to get to know their students and how they learn best. They discover what motivates them and what makes them feel inadequate. However, oftentimes when teachers share their findings from this authentic assessment and suggest a solution that's best for the individual student, they're told that the child doesn't qualify for services or that resources are unavailable. Resources are low and expectations are high, yet much of the data that teachers are responsible for collecting is not leading to the support children really need.

Is It Playtime Yet?

As we continue to push our children to race to the top, we find ourselves wondering why it is that they can't seem to sit still, follow the rules, or get along with others. Our children spend less and less time playing outdoors and more and more time sitting at their desks struggling through assessments. Gone are the days when teachers were able to spend the first six weeks of the school year establishing classroom rules, teaching kids to get along with one another, and practicing the art of problem solving. These days, we are so busy testing our students and collecting data on them that we've been forced to cut the most important lessons of all—believe in yourself and speak your truth. And what about learning through play? With so much pressure on teachers to ensure their students are meeting test-score standards, there's little time for free or even organized play.

At the beginning of first grade, my son came to me and firmly stated: "It's just not fair, Mom. I'm only in first grade, and I never get to play. All we do is work, work, and more work." It saddens me to hear this, because play is one of the greatest learning tools children have. And when we fill young students' days with too much programming and structure, we deprive them of this great opportunity to learn and grow both socially and emotionally.

In his 1986 work *All I Really Need to Know I Learned in Kindergarten*, minister and author Robert Fulghum artfully depicts the lessons learned in kindergarten as life guidance that should never be forgotten. Some of these include *share everything, play fair,* and *say you're sorry when you hurt somebody.* My personal favorite was "live a balanced life—learn some and think some and draw and paint and sing and dance and work every day some." Unfortunately, our kids are missing out on this lesson and so much more when we rush them through their childhood with an excessive amount of testing and data collection. We are far too busy trying to categorize our children and measuring their successes (or failures) to notice that what they *really* need is to be seen, heard, accepted, honored, supported, and guided with unconditional love, so that they can *be* their absolute best and shine that inner light.

If we truly want to teach our children effectively, we need to begin by touching their hearts before we even attempt to teach their minds. Children have an innate love for learning, but they will not open their minds to you unless they trust you. Sure, they will learn some of the curriculum by default, but if we are aiming for our children to learn *depth instead of breadth*—a deep understanding instead of surface learning—then we need to *connect* with them. We need to get to know them and allow them to know us. We need to accept them and teach them to accept others. In a system where we are focused on data collection and number analysis, we lose connection and ultimately diminish our children's natural love of learning.

If we continue to spend so much time testing our children instead of building character and teaching them how to tap into the wonder of learning, we are dimming their light instead of igniting it. The anxiety created by this "race to the top" and "leave no child behind" mentality is causing children and teachers to feel inadequate. This increases the frustration of both students and teachers and leads us down a road full of fear. When demands increase and children feel inadequate, they lash out at one another; and before you know it, you have a bullying crisis on your hands.

On September 13, 2010, New York State signed into law the Dignity for All Students Act (commonly referred to as the Dignity Act), and it took effect on July 1, 2012. According to the state department of education, the act "seeks to provide the State's public elementary and secondary school students with a safe and supportive environment free from discrimination, intimidation, taunting, harassment, and bullying on school property, a school bus and/or at a school function." Many schools across New York State are now implementing new bullying programs in line with the mandate. But I believe they're failing to see the big picture. We are causing a great deal of the frustration and stress these students are feeling, and we're not teaching them the skills they need to cope with these feelings or to thrive in spite of them. Of course they are going to lash out at one another. A bully is generally a person who feels inadequate or lacking in some way. If we spent more of our time connecting with our children (seeing their magnificence) and less time evaluating them (categorizing their failures and successes), perhaps bullying wouldn't be the enormous problem it is today.

Children are experiencing stress at a much younger age, and it's leading to poor socialization skills and health problems. Educators are also experiencing high levels of stress, leading them down the same road. The pressure to document effective teaching strategies while planning interesting, thought-provoking, differentiated instruction that meets the current standards of education for all students is becoming almost impossible to handle. There is little time for collaborating with fellow teachers and creating units of study to pique student interest, yet we wonder why our children are not easily engaged and are struggling in school.

Behind Closed Doors

Sadly, the education system isn't the only area where we're overlooking the importance of childhood. Within the home, many children spend more time engaging with electronics than they do engaging with real people. They aren't playing outside like they used to, and quality family time has become a foreign concept to many. We have reached a point where family members may be sitting in the same room together, but instead of enjoying each other's company, they're busy playing on Facebook, searching the Web, or answering e-mails on electronic handheld devices. We are raising the "iGeneration," and I'm not so sure that's a good thing. Technology *can* be amazing, but we seem to have lost sight of moderation.

Parents are working hard to support their children and give them everything that they never had. Regrettably, much of their focus is centered on the material things in life instead of matters of the heart. Like their children, parents are pulled in many different directions and feel that there is just not enough time. We live in a busy, fast-paced world and in order to keep up we often find ourselves returning e-mails, texting, talking on the phone, or sitting in front of a computer while our children are by our sides. We adults spend an awful lot of time in our heads and not a lot of time connected to our hearts. This isn't intentional. We're simply trying to keep up. But while we're treading water in this way, we are missing the messages that our children are sending. We're disconnected from their true feelings because we're not in touch with our own emotions. Of course, our lack of connection teaches our children how to disconnect—from themselves and from each other—which can only lead to more problems.

Most people have a tendency to spend significant amounts of time thinking about the past, especially the events that have caused stress or heartache, and a good deal of time dreaming about the future. Consequently, we don't spend enough time in the present moment. It's fair to say that most of us are *mind full* but not *mindful*. In other words, our minds are cluttered with thoughts, yet we aren't taking time to quiet our minds, connect to our hearts, and ignite our own light.

When it comes to responsibilities, we take on too much and do far more than anyone needs to in any given day. We unfortunately forget that we are human *beings* instead of human *doings*. We get it in our heads that if we do more, then we'll be more successful and able to provide more for our families. The truth is, when we do too much, we lose contact with who we truly are and we ignore the most important part of our being—our higher self. We totally disconnect from our inner light and put on our tunnel-vision goggles in order to simply make it through our days. It's as if we aren't truly living, but instead just existing.

The heartbreaking part of all this is that we aren't deliberately setting out to harm our children or minimize the importance of childhood. Instead, it's as though we're sleepwalking. We seem to be completely unaware that life's critical moments are passing us by. Before you know it, the child you once held in your arms or the little ones who looked to you for guidance are all grown up and burdened by baggage you never intended to send out into the world with them.

Do *you* ever feel as though you're walking around in a haze and simply *doing* life instead of living? If so, it's not too late to do something about it. You *can* make a positive change. You *can* create a strong foundation for your children by igniting the light within them—but first you must become aware and take a look at your own foundation.

Your Foundation

Just for a moment, imagine your life as a building. What if you were in charge of creating this massive structure from the planning stages to its physical manifestation? Imagine, what would it take to create a strong, safe, and enduring building that would last a lifetime? First, you might consider talking with an experienced architect—one who knew the ins and outs of creating such an edifice. You would want to find an expert who could help you to turn your vision into a reality. You might begin by sitting down with this authority and explaining your ideas in full detail. The architect would most certainly design a blueprint according to your vision, while also making sure that all of the right stuff was in place so that the building could last a lifetime. The next logical step would include getting the building supplies together. Only the strongest and best materials would do.

In order to actually manifest this structure you would need workers. The workers begin the same way on every building they create: they lay the *foundation*. This is truly the most important part of the whole process because if the foundation is weak, then the building will not last. If that foundation begins to crack or crumble during construction, then the structure is likely to be a danger to society at some point in time. Finally, if the foundation has critical issues that aren't repaired, the building will eventually become idle. It will never truly reach its full potential.

In general, all workers are given the same materials to create a building. They all begin with some type of steel and concrete, and then they use wood, nails, glue, and so on. Oftentimes, those workers are underpaid, undernourished, and extremely tired, so they don't necessarily follow the blueprint. In fact, they may not even know that the blueprint exists! The mason comes in and works with stones and concrete. The carpenters create the wood structures. The electricians handle the electrical grid. The designers come in to perform their jobs, and on and on. Each of the workers does what they know how to do. They don't necessarily know about the overall blueprint or perhaps even care about it because they are simply doing what *they* learned how to do. Consequently, while your vision began with a blueprint, it may veer slightly off course as the project unfolds.

Now, you might ask yourself, *What does this building that I've created in my mind have to do with my life—and more important, with igniting the light within children?*

Building the Future

Remember that the building that you created in your mind is actually a metaphor for your life. The architect is none other than your higher power (God). The blueprint is the plan that you may have made with God prior to birth for what you are currently living. That means that the *workers* were the people who raised you or had critical input during your childhood (your teachers, religious leaders, relatives, and so on) and the *foundation* was everything that you were given and taught in childhood that makes you who you are today.

Did you ever stop to think that perhaps everything that we create in this life is something that we have thought prior to its manifestation? I've learned from years of self-reflection and spiritual deepening that we do, in fact, think the thoughts that bring our destiny to us: bad, good, and indifferent. When you think something, feel it, and truly believe that it is so, you energetically attract just that into your being. Divine energy is like a parent who simply allows, and never says no to your desires. If you think, *I am scared,* then the Universe says, *Okay!* And, guess what you are? That's right, scared. If you think, *I am loved,* then the Universe says, *Okay!* And you are loved. You cannot be denied what you truly wish to experience, because that's *your free will.*

Perhaps we all have a plan before we enter this life. Maybe you wondered, imagined, and began to create your journey long before you were born. Some of us may have come to this life to experience forgiveness. Some may be on a path to right a wrong. Some may be here to learn unconditional love. We each arrive with lessons, or a *blueprint,* that we predetermine with God, Divine Energy, or a higher power. It doesn't matter what you call this energy. The only thing that matters is that you recognize that we are all a part of something much bigger than ourselves.

I've always believed that we have a plan before birth, but it was my son who validated this belief for me. We were sitting at the kitchen table playing with Play-Doh when he was four years old, and he enlightened me with his amazing wisdom. We were simply playing and laughing when I noticed that he was staring at me and smiling.

I looked at him directly and asked, "Nico, what are you smiling at?"

He responded, "I'm so happy that I picked you, Mommy."

I smiled with an inquisitive look upon my face and continued our conversation by saying, "Picked me? What do you mean, buddy?"

He grabbed my hand and said, "You know, when I was up in heaven with God. I picked you because you're beautiful, Mommy. You have a really bright light!"

Words cannot explain how stunned I was. I felt tingles run up my spine, and I knew that he was expressing his truth right before my eyes. Interestingly, we do not practice a religion in our home. I've never really talked about heaven, per se. When Nico asks questions, I simply ask him to tell me what he thinks, and we continue our discussion from there. So, I know when he mentioned "heaven," he was speaking his truth!

A few weeks after this experience with my son, I pulled out a terrific book to read to him at bedtime. This children's book by Neale Donald Walsch, *The Little Soul and the Sun,* is perhaps one of the most enlightening stories I've ever read. It describes beautifully how we choose our lessons here on Earth before we are born. At the end of the book, my son looked at me and said, "See, I told you. That's kind of how I picked you!" Well, what is it they say? "Out of the mouths of babes!"

This particular book and my experience with my son are perfect examples of a *blueprint* in motion. This plan that you co-created with God (or whomever you consider your higher power) is the Divine record of what you wanted to learn in this life. Maybe you wanted to learn forgiveness. Perhaps you wanted to learn humility. Look at your life and the lessons you've had so far and really begin to go within to see what is revealed to you. Is there a theme that keeps coming back? The *blueprint* is what came from your meeting with the almighty architect. It has helped you to create your building, which is your life. You know that you are on course with your blueprint when you *feel* as if you are in the flow and things move along smoothly. This happens when you have tapped into your inner light.

The *workers,* or the people who raised you or directly came in contact with you during your early life, impact how your blueprint unfolds. The workers are simply doing the best they can, given their specific skills and qualifications. When a child is born, no one hands you a manual and says, "Here you go. Here's your instruction manual for this particular model." While it might be helpful to get such a manual, it wouldn't necessarily help the child learn the lessons he or she came here to learn.

When I am working with clients in my coaching practice, our first order of business is to get to the core beliefs that are holding them back. Many times, people want to place all the blame on their parents or caregivers. But true healing only comes from understanding that we are all doing the best that we can with what we have to work with. Your parents, caregivers, and teachers, never truly intended to harm you, although it certainly may appear that way at times. They were simply doing their job based upon the *foundation* that they were given as children.

Tools for Success

Because childhood is so brief, it is imperative that we use the time to provide our children with the tools for success that they can access the rest of their lives. Childhood *is* our foundation because it launches us toward everything that follows. It is within this time period that our core beliefs are formed. We carry these beliefs throughout our lives, and they're responsible for setting our journeys in motion. They also influence the thoughts we have on a daily basis. These thoughts circle back and deepen our core beliefs, and finally create our experiences. By realizing that you're born with a blueprint, you can begin to understand how to read, follow, and make adjustments to it as needed, so that you can be your absolute best self mentally, physically, and emotionally. In

Part II of this book you will learn the *7 Essentials* that will give you a new frame of mind. When you ignite the light within, you bring out your very best. When you're your best self, then you are ready to create the strong foundation that your children so desperately need and desire. A strong foundation is one that has essential tools to help you to *live* instead of merely existing. Your mental, emotional, and overall worldview depends on the quality of this foundation that was created in childhood.

With every decision we make and each action we take, our children become immersed in lessons and learn from us. They learn how to react or respond to life. They learn what to think and what to believe. Unfortunately, they sometimes learn how to silence the voice within that gently guides them back to their blueprint when they go off course. Awareness is the first step to change. If we become aware of the importance of childhood, then we can begin to change our children's current curriculum. You don't necessarily have to be a certified teacher to do this. You're actually teaching a daily curriculum by simply living *your* life, because children are always watching, listening, and learning. With this knowledge, you can begin to make positive changes by improving your plan of instruction.

Perhaps we have been too busy to remain mindful of this critical time period called childhood. Maybe we, as a society, have too much going on to notice what our children really need. They may be lacking in social, emotional, and communication skills because we're spending too much time focused on data collection and not enough time on making connections. But it's not too late to shift gears.

We have the power to create strong foundations for our children. As parents and educators we have an incredible opportunity to teach our children just how amazing they are while they're still young and impressionable. This is our chance to give them the tools to be successful in life while teaching them how to tap into the beautiful light within. Giving our children a strong foundation means giving them the tools to communicate their feelings effectively, speak their truth, and love and accept themselves just as they are. It's empowering them to embrace the belief that we are all connected. Wouldn't all of this be a terrific way to start your journey in life?

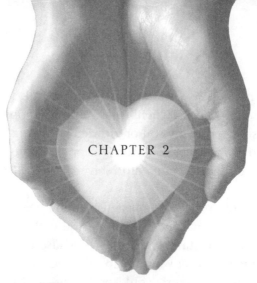

CHAPTER 2

THROUGH THE EYES OF A CHILD

*"Seek the wisdom of the ages, but look
at the world through the eyes of a child."*

— RON WILD

On a Monday afternoon in late September, we had a faculty meeting that left all of us teachers in a state of panic. Due to imminent changes to the American education system, we were all feeling pressure: administrators, teachers, and most sadly, the students. As we walked out of that meeting, you could cut the tension with a plastic knife. We were now being asked to document more of our teaching throughout the day, write up lengthy lesson plans for observations, and do even more testing and data collection. I have to admit, I was a bit fired up that evening. I was worried about how I would fit more into the already jam-packed school day. But despite the way the meeting had left me feeling, I was able to let the negativity go. I hopped in my car, drove home, and greeted my family with the most genuine smile I could muster given the circumstances. There were certainly moments where I could have snapped at my son or growled at my husband, but instead I found a way to let go of the tension, knowing there wasn't much I could do in that moment to solve all the issues our schools were facing.

It turned out one of my colleagues hadn't been so lucky. The next morning, I went into school a little earlier than usual. I hoped to get a jump-start on my day while also trying to develop a bit of a game plan that would help me cope with the imminent requirements we educators would be facing. As I was preparing a document for my morning lesson, my colleague Karen, whose classroom was adjacent to mine, passed by in a noticeable rush. I gave her a few minutes and then spouted my usual good-morning call. Typically, she responded to my jovial greeting with a joke of her own, but this day was different. I called out her name and waited for a reply, but there was no response. I called out again, but she still wasn't answering, so I stood up and walked purposefully into her room. I noticed that she was choking back tears, trying not to let them materialize. I looked at her with caring eyes and inquired as to how I could help. Within a few minutes she opened up to me about the challenging morning she'd had.

A mom to twin four-year-old girls, Karen had been living through the developmental stage known as *executive competence*, which basically means, "I'll do it my own way, Mommy!" While one of the twins is fairly easygoing and generally listens when asked to do something, the other is what you might label a strong-willed child. She has more difficulty following directions without first questioning the request. On this particular morning, my colleague had woken up late because she'd been worked up from the staff meeting the evening before and had trouble falling asleep. She was rushing around to get the girls ready for school and could already feel her stress levels rising with the mounting pressure of being late. She laid out clothes for the girls and asked them to get dressed while she continued her morning tasks. This apparently led to a major power struggle. If you have children, you likely know this story all too well. The T-shirt is red instead of pink. The pants are too tight. The socks don't feel right. And let's not forget: "I'm just too tired to get dressed." We've all experienced mornings like this, and they seem to hit the hardest when we're strapped for time or short on patience.

It appeared as though anything that could have gone wrong for Karen that morning had. By the time she got her kids in the car, they were all in a complete tizzy. Her strong-willed daughter chose that moment to shout something along the lines of "You're a mean mommy and you don't even love me!" Karen completely lost it. By the time she got to work, she was so emotionally drained that no matter how hard she tried, she simply couldn't stop herself from crying. She felt like a complete failure and couldn't understand how the day had started off so badly and her emotions had taken over so quickly.

When she finished telling me the story with tears streaming down her face, I looked at her and smiled warmly. Karen's daughter, the one who appears to fight her on everything, had experienced health problems at the start of her life and constantly needed more attention and care than her twin sister. The little girl's medical issues had become less severe with age, but she still required additional support and certain precautions had to be taken. She struggled with learning, had difficulty making decisions, and had a tough time feeling comfortable in social situations. Her twin sister, on the other hand, excelled in school, made friends easily, and was at the top of all of the developmental charts.

That morning Karen and I spoke about her daughter and the reasons behind her defiant behavior. I pointed out that she was probably feeling inadequate and struggling to communicate. This was all part of her *blueprint*—and stemmed back to her first days of life. The behaviors she was exhibiting were most likely the result of these feelings of inadequacy. The resistance around clothing was probably a result of her not feeling good enough in her own skin. Her health issues and need for additional support and attention likely gave her the feeling that she was broken or needed fixing. She probably had trouble following directions because she was fearful that she wouldn't "get it right." How could she not compare herself to her twin? It must have been difficult for one sister to struggle with so much when the other seemed to get things so easily.

As we talked, Karen began to realize that she had contributed to the morning chaos by carrying over her stress from the previous day. She had been too preoccupied to recognize what her daughter was *really* feeling that morning. But, I reminded her: "You're human. You're entitled to *react* to life once in a while. Just try not to make a habit of it."

Karen's stress coupled with her daughter's insecurities was a perfect recipe for disaster that morning. But the experience was a really good opportunity for my colleague to see how directly her own energy impacted that of her children. We talked for a few more minutes about the differences between reacting and responding to situations in life before the morning welcome announcement came over the loud speaker. Karen smiled and said, "Okay, Savini, now how bad do I look? Can you tell I was crying?" As always, I had a smart-ass remark for her before leaving the room. I was certainly pleased to look back and see her smiling as I crossed over into my classroom area.

Karen hadn't set out to create a belief within her daughter that she wasn't good enough. But when a baby is born with health issues and almost doesn't make it, it's hard to avoid heaping that fear and worry onto the child. The terror of losing a child is breathtaking for any parent, and when you see that your child is ailing or has a special need, you want more than anything to meet that need or take away the hurt. Unfortunately, because of early health concerns and the amount of necessary additional care, this child began to believe that she was broken. Because she required extra support, she internalized the belief that she must rely on others instead of herself. Although these beliefs had already been formed, I was sure that with a little care and attention, this little girl could grow up to be as self-assured and confident as her twin sister. It would, however, require some awareness on the part of her mother.

On any given day in a crowded place, you can find a child sitting in awe—watching and taking in all that is going on around them. As we adults go about our lives, we often don't stop to realize that children are watching, listening, and learning from our actions. They're paying closer attention than we often think, processing our behaviors and storing them away in their memories. Even when our children are sleeping, they are still learning from us because they're replaying the day over in their heads and making sense of the world around them. As we're busy living our lives, they are watching and internalizing our actions and *reactions* to the world. We are setting a continuous example: what to do, how to feel, and how to handle life in general.

Once you become aware that this is going on, you'll be more conscious of your choices and reactions. You'll feel more empowered to make a difference in the life of a child by focusing more on the lessons you're teaching through your own behaviors. When we become more mindful of what our children are learning from us, we can begin to inspire and empower them in ways we never imagined possible.

No Use Crying Over Spilled Dirt

My dad was truly an amazing man. He was a rock for my mom, my sisters, and me. His grandchildren adored him, and everywhere he went children were drawn to him. He had a huge smile and a light within that was like a magnet. He was the type of guy who would give a perfect stranger the shirt off of his back or the last dollar in his pocket if he felt that they needed it more than he did. He was a problem solver: when others were in a state of panic, he was always three steps ahead, thinking about how to resolve the crisis as it unfolded. It was as if he saw things right before they would happen. As a child, I always thought the sun rose and set on my dad. He was kind, caring, fun, and insightful. He could always make me laugh, no matter how down I was feeling. Dad was my go-to guy. And I assumed every father was like that.

It wasn't until I grew up that I began to realize my dad saw things differently because he could see the world through the eyes of a child.

My dad believed that kids should be allowed to just be kids: they should laugh, play, and discover the world around them while being protected and loved unconditionally by their tribe (or family). He felt that their boundless energy should be embraced instead of harnessed. Dad was a thinker, but more important, he *felt* life's experiences very deeply. Perhaps that's why he brought a sense of calm whenever he was around. He had the gift of knowing what the children around him were feeling, which ultimately made their thoughts apparent as well. Even though he was an adult, he continued to see things as a child would—and I proudly inherited that from him.

My dad was typically centered in love. My mom, on the other hand, was always overwhelmed by fear. I distinctly remember a time in my early 20s when I was still living with my mom and dad. Four of my six nieces and nephews were in the early stages of childhood: there was one seven-year-old, two spunky five-year-olds, and a three-year-old who completed the crew. Early one morning when I was in my room drying my hair, I heard a crash in a nearby room and stopped the blow-dryer for a moment to listen closer. I tuned in to the kids' soft whispers, which were quickly rising to a rumble of panic.

Jason, who was the eldest, said, "Uh-oh, that's a big one!" Then I heard some mumbling and nervous whispers once again.

Sammy Jo said, "Who are we gonna tell? We can't let Nana know, she'll freak!"

Jason replied, "Nuni will know what to do!" (Nuni is short for *nuna*, which means godmother in Greek. I acquired this name as Jason's godmother because his father is Greek, and he was baptized in the Greek church.)

A few seconds later, I heard little fists quietly, yet frantically, knocking on my door.

I felt needed and honored because they had turned to me at a time of sheer panic. I believe that they had chosen to come to me because they knew I would listen to them, hear what had happened, and help them to come up with a solution without judgment. They were certain that I wasn't going to "freak." Why? Because children pick up on other people's energy quite easily. They instinctively know who is full of fear (reacting to life) and who is full of love (able to respond).

The catastrophe was an easy one to solve. Little Arianna had knocked a plant over when they were chasing each other through the dining room, and her older brother Jason was willing to take the blame for it. We talked about it, and I assured them that there was no use in crying over spilled dirt! We cleaned it up together, just as my mom returned from the grocery store with my sister and promptly asked, "What happened here?"

Jason replied, "Nothin', Nana. Nuni's takin' care of it."

My mom glared at me inquisitively and I responded, "Yes, Mom. We've got it all under control. There's nothing to worry about."

When I think back to this day, I still feel honored knowing that my nieces and nephews had looked to me as their refuge. They knew I was a safe adult who "got it" and who would respond to their mishap with love instead of fear.

My mother isn't a terrible mom or nana. She's just so full of fear that it's hard for her to respond to life in a loving way. Her childhood was full of fear and as a result, she raised her children in a cloud of worry. The cracks in my mom's foundation caused her to be cautious and fearful, always wondering when the other shoe would drop. Years ago, when I began looking within for answers to my own challenges from childhood, I realized that my mom had really meant no harm. But it's hard to explain that to a child, especially when they're feeling guilty for making a mistake, like knocking over a plant.

Life is actually pretty simple. We are all driven by two forces —love and fear. You know that fear is in charge when you're stuck in your head. Your thoughts take you on a downward spiral of negativity, and one fearful thought leads directly into the next. When we are caught up in fear, we aren't present in the current moment. We're running from our past or chasing the future. It's easy to snap at children when we're in this state, because we aren't mindful of how they're interpreting our behavior or what they're learning from us. When you're in a state of panic, everything else becomes a blur and you start *reacting* to life.

On the flip side, when love is at the helm, you are centered in your heart. You go by what *feels* right instead of what you've been told is right. You make decisions based upon the feeling within your body as opposed to the thoughts in your head. When you're motivated by love, you take the time to *respond* to life instead reacting to its circumstances.

React or Respond? That Is the Question

As adults, we think we can hide our feelings from our children, but the truth is we can't. Even if we're good actors, children know that something is not right because they emotionally *sense* our energy long before we actually react. Before they have time to process what is happening psychologically or even physically, their emotional senses take over. I know this to be true as a mother and a teacher. It never fails that behavior appears to be off in the classroom or at home when I feel unbalanced or stressed out myself. It took me a while to recognize this, but the truth is, the little people in front of me are reading my energy and mirroring it right back to me. You can look at this as a curse or a blessing. I personally believe that it helps me to be my best self for them, and I hope that you will feel the same.

When we are feeling stressed about money, work, or the daily grind, the downloads from our past play louder and louder: *You're not good enough, you'll never amount to anything, good things don't happen to people like you, you're not smart enough, who do you think you are?* As the voices rise to a crescendo, our thoughts go into overdrive and we begin to feel completely off balance. We have so many thoughts racing through our minds at one time that we become stuck in a cloud of fear. It is often at this very moment that a child steps in and demands our attention or tests our patience. Because we're being driven by fear, we react. It's really that simple. When we're stuck in our heads instead of our hearts we often react to life in a knee-jerk manner. We don't take a breath before speaking because we're caught up in all those thoughts of fear. It is as if we have been dropped in the ocean of life, and all we can think about is keeping our head above water. Unfortunately, while we're in the water struggling to stay afloat, our children are watching, listening, learning, and mimicking our actions.

We all have moments when we're caught up in fear and, as a result, we react to life. I remember a time when this happened to me, and I felt myself reacting to a student's behavior in a negative way. Luckily, I was able to become conscious of what I was doing and shift my reaction to a response—just in the nick of time.

Bella was a beautiful little girl who was quite accustomed to getting her own way. I remember being handed her kindergarten information card and told that she could be quite the handful. I smiled and put the card away in my filing cabinet, believing that I'd rather get to know this student first and form my own opinions of her. But, I could see within the first few weeks of school why Bella had this reputation. She certainly had a mind of her own and didn't particularly like to follow directions. In spite of this, she and I got along quite well and had a mutual understanding of how things ran in our classroom. Bella's mom was a kind, caring parent who was active in her child's life. When I met her, she immediately shared with me that Bella's dad passed on unexpectedly when the little girl was only eight months old and that it had been just the two of them ever since. I could see the pain in her mother's eyes as she shared the story, and I felt deep sadness for both Bella and her mom. It was clear that there was some guilt being experienced by her mother as well. And as I got to know Bella and her mom better, it became evident that Bella ran the show, so to speak.

Following the winter break, I started to notice Bella exhibiting some defiant behavior. I talked with her mom at length to come up with a behavior plan and stressed the importance of following through at home. Bella was a smart little girl and knew that she needed to be a good listener and follow directions in order to earn her reward, yet the plan wasn't working. I knew there must be something deeper going on—so I went out on a limb. It was the middle of the week (likely close to a full moon) when Bella's plea for help came shining through. Everywhere that Bella went, I received reports of defiant behavior. She wasn't listening to other teachers during "specials" (subjects such as art and music), she was talking back to the recess monitor, and she was disappearing from the lunchroom at will.

Finally, I sat her down for a one-on-one chat. I spoke with her about her behaviors and explained why they weren't safe. She was more mindful for about five minutes—until she went into the hallway and caused a bit of havoc in the girls bathroom. She was promptly brought back to me by yet another teacher in the building. My main concern was her lack of remorse for her actions. She really didn't seem bothered by getting into all of this trouble, which to me was a true sign of a cry for help. I contacted her mom at work and asked if we could meet for an impromptu parent-teacher-child conference that day after school. Her mom shared that she had been seeing the same behaviors at home and getting reports from day care as well. She too was concerned with Bella's lack of remorse.

In our school we have a mentor program where adults in our building serve as experienced and trusted advisors for students in need. One of our physical education coaches was Bella's mentor, acting as a father figure for her from the time she entered school. Immediately following dismissal that day, Bella went to my classroom with her mentor while I greeted her mother in the school lobby. Prior to entering the classroom, her mom expressed concern that she had done something wrong as a parent because her child didn't seem to care about being reprimanded and showed no remorse for her actions. She worried that she hadn't properly bonded with Bella as a baby, because she'd been so overwhelmed first with postpartum depression and then with clinical depression following the loss of her husband. Bella's mom was very concerned about what this might mean for her daughter's future, and felt that she was failing as a mother. It was at that moment I realized this mother was driven completely by fear, and Bella was simply mirroring it. I assured her that we would get through this together and that her daughter loved her and did in fact feel connected to her. This was evident to me on a daily basis.

As we entered the room, Bella was smiling and giddy, even though she knew that her mom was coming for a meeting based on inappropriate behavior. Her mother was sickened and emotionally distraught, yet she greeted her daughter with warmth. As we sat together at the table, Bella said everything she thought we wanted to hear. With a smirk, she calmly stated, "I know we're having this meeting because of my behavior. I'm not making good choices and I need to be a better listener. I'm sorry, Mommy."

Her mom sat there with tears streaming down her face, and Bella was still half smiling.

I looked directly into her wise six-year old-eyes and said, "Bella, thank you for telling us what we'd like to hear, but now I'd like to know how you *feel.* Can you put both hands on your heart and close your eyes?" She nodded her head and followed my directions. I continued, "Now tell me what you are *feeling.* I don't want you to tell me the words you've heard us say. Instead, I want to know what it feels like inside your heart right now."

I referred to my children's book, *The Light Inside of Me,* because I use that often with my students, and she was familiar with the concept. I asked her if her light was dim or bright and if she could use an "I Statement" to tell me why.

She opened her eyes and her whole demeanor changed. She gently tilted her head to one side and said, "Well, Mrs. Savini, I feel lonely. Sometimes I just wish that one of my friends could live at my house because I am really lonely and that makes me feel sad. Sometimes I wish I had a different life because I just feel sad."

At this point, we all had tears in our eyes because we realized that her defiant behavior had been, in fact, a cry for help.

Prior to this, the plan had been to meet with Bella and give her a serious consequence for her actions in the hopes that she would change her behavior and all would be well. This, I realized, was a poor plan because we were simply *reacting* to her with fear instead of *responding* to her needs. We didn't want her to misbehave anymore, and we wanted her to understand the importance of following directions and being a good listener, for her safety and that of others. We were annoyed by her crass attitude and lack of remorse. But the reality was, we were viewing a child in pain. After hearing her speak her truth, it became evident that she didn't need a consequence at all. What she needed was to feel noticed, loved, and valued. Instead of reacting to the situation, we responded. By asking Bella to feel her feelings and talk about them, we were able to get to the root of the defiant behaviors. Although her mother spent all of her spare time with Bella and provided well for her, the new plan meant that Mom would spend more *quality* time with her daughter and arrange for play dates so that she could spend more time with children her own age.

That day I saw a light ignite within Bella *and* her mom. After the meeting, the mother promptly turned to me and said, "I get it, Mrs. Savini. I totally get it. Just being there and taking care of her isn't enough. She needs me to connect with her, even if it's just making dinner together. I totally get it now." An outsider would look at Bella and see a child who was well taken care of and possibly a bit spoiled. Yet Bella believed that she wasn't important, and she was feeling a bit invisible. The family made some simple changes, and within a short period of time Bella was a whole new child—her best self.

After our meeting in the classroom, Bella's mom reached out to me for coaching because she recognized the importance of healing the child within her, so that she could be the best mom for her daughter. We worked together for several months to uncover the core beliefs that were causing her to create exactly what she didn't want in her relationship with her daughter. I am proud to say that both ladies are thriving today.

Energy Mirrors

Our children are mirrors for whatever we're experiencing in life. While we may think we're hiding our troubles well, we almost certainly are not. Children feel the energy we project. In the case of my co-worker Karen, her daughter had nothing to do with the stress that her mom woke up with in the morning. She couldn't possibly have known that Mommy was carrying tension from her job and feeling pressured about a late start. Karen also wasn't aware of the energy she was projecting onto her daughter. She woke up, her feet hit the ground, and she was off and running. She wasn't mindful of her feelings or centered in her own energy when she greeted her children. As a result, it was inevitable that something would go wrong that morning. Events continued in a downward spiral because Karen's energy was setting the stage for the day. She had already woken up feeling stressed and inadequate, so when her daughter said she wasn't a good mom, it struck a nerve or underlying belief that "I'm not good enough." Unfortunately, the child could also see her mom worrying that she wasn't enough. She could pick up on that fear. The twins weren't just experiencing "Crazy Mommy" that morning (and you know we've all been there); instead, they were learning how fear drives us to react. This is why her daughter gave her such a hard time. She saw Mommy acting out of fear, and she mirrored that behavior. The energy triggered her *own* fears of inadequacy.

Bella was doing the same thing. Her mom was walking around with a fear that she wasn't good enough to be her mother. The mother carried that weight on her shoulders, feeling that she and her daughter had never properly bonded. She gave in to the girl's every whim in the hopes of being accepted as a mom. This gave Bella more power than any six-year-old should have, and made her feel unimportant because there were no consistent boundaries. The mother wasn't responding to her child or her needs, because she was reacting to her own inner fears instead. She feared that she didn't have a strong connection with her daughter, while what the daughter was aching for was that true connection. A behavior plan wouldn't have worked for Bella because all she wanted was to connect with her mother, to feel loved, noticed, and important. Mom wasn't saying the words, "You're not important," "You're invisible," or "You're not loved," but that was Bella's perception. When we took the time to shift from fear to love, we were able to hear what was missing right from Bella's lips. We were then able to meet the need and promptly shift a negative behavior pattern and prevent further damage.

When children give us a hard time, we're quick to judge their behavior as "bad" or "defiant," but the truth is, they have learned this behavior from us somewhere along the line or they have developed it as a means to hide emotional pain they feel within. By default, we often teach our children the exact opposite of what we want them to be or what we expect them to do. Remember that we are consciously and unconsciously teaching our children a daily curriculum by simply living our lives. The true power comes from choosing your curriculum wisely. Will you teach your children how to *react* to life or *respond* to life? In Part II of this book, you will learn about the 7 essentials I teach children and adults. These essentials will help you to gain a different perspective so that you can respond to life and teach children how to do the same. The material we teach our children determines the core beliefs that they carry throughout their lifetime. What's your curriculum composed of—love or fear?

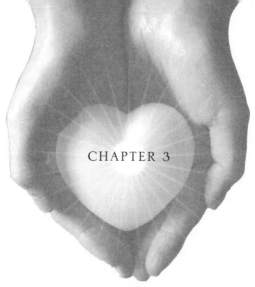

CHAPTER 3

CORE BELIEFS

"A belief is only a thought I continue to think."

— ABRAHAM (ESTHER AND JERRY HICKS)

My first college experience was not a good one. I moved an hour and a half away from home to attend school in the hopes of becoming an art teacher. At the time, I really wasn't sure what I wanted out of life, but I knew that I wanted to work with children and I'd been told that I was a talented artist. After securing a sizable scholarship for this particular program, I felt encouraged that combining my love of children with my artistic talent was a good idea. I didn't necessarily want to be away from my family, but at the time I felt that this was what I needed to do in order to grow and expand.

But none of it worked out as I'd expected. I was miserable at this school. My roommate was pleasant, but her friends were classic "mean girls." I had struggled with fitting in my entire life because I'd always felt a bit unlike everyone else. My experience at college was no different. Looking back, I now realize that the reason why I felt so out of place my whole life was because I was a "connected child"—one who hears the voice within loud and clear. The problem was that I didn't have parents or a mentor who could explain what I was experiencing, and so I questioned that voice instead of tuning in and trusting. No one in my inner circle helped me to understand the importance of listening to my inner voice or making sense of the feelings I was experiencing. I knew what I knew, but I didn't understand my own insight. This was part of the reason I wanted to go away to school. My hope was to find others who were like me. Imagine my disappointment when I landed in a program where mean girls invaded my privacy and devoured what little self-esteem I had left.

I felt lost studying art, because while I had won several awards and been told that I was a terrific artist, I didn't think I was good enough and never felt like I fit in at the studio. These feelings of unworthiness and the sense that I didn't belong brought on an awful bout of depression. I spoke with my parents daily and begged to come home. My parents guided me as best as they could and encouraged me to seek professional help on campus. I did what I was told, but desperately wanted to quit school and move back home.

After one semester of suffering, I got out of there and enrolled in a college in my hometown. It was a prestigious school and actually ranked higher than the one I left, but that didn't matter to me because I was still plagued by my feelings of inadequacy. I felt like a failure, running home instead of finishing what I'd started. This new college didn't have an arts program, so I had to be creative with my choice of degrees in order to hold on to my coveted scholarship that would lead to me becoming a teacher. I enrolled in the political science program with a minor in education. My hope was to change the world and keep my scholarship.

Thankfully I felt much more welcome in this new environment. Even though I was starting in the second semester, many of the students and faculty went out of their way to make me feel at ease. I was invited to visit the campus prior to the start of classes and assigned a school ambassador to show me around. This is how I met my dear friend Eileen, affectionately referred to as Chaloopah. Eileen was a sweet Colombian girl with an inviting smile and an outgoing personality. I met her in the early morning and was scheduled to be with her until dinnertime. I could tell from the moment we met that she was a bright light. Her inner beauty totally outshone her outer beauty—and she was quite an attractive young woman. At first, I felt uncomfortable because she was so outgoing and everyone seemed to know and love her. I was desperate to fit in and feeling a bit self-conscious, and this made me feel even more insecure. I think she must have recognized this, because she quickly took me under her wing and introduced me to just about every soul on campus.

I had been dreading this campus tour because I was painfully nervous that everyone would sense my depression and that I once again would feel like an outcast. However, by dinnertime, when we were supposed to part, I really didn't want to go. I saw my dad pull up to the curb and I quickly turned to Eileen and said, "Why don't you come to dinner with me? I guarantee my Italian mom can give you a meal better than campus slop!" She laughed and graciously accepted. Then we hopped in the car. After introducing my dad to Eileen and seeing his beaming smile—because he knew instinctively that my inner light was slowly reigniting—I suddenly realized that Eileen was on her way to *my* house and I began to panic. My family was, and still is, the typical Italian-American family. If you know anything about Italian-Americans, you know that they are often loud and speak without a filter. I got quieter as we rode home. I worried about what my new friend would think of my family—and as a result, me.

My mom welcomed us with a big hug and tons of questions. We enjoyed a nice Italian dinner with my mom, dad, and one of my three sisters, before cleaning up, engaging in a full-on water fight (both in and out of the house, much to my mother's dismay), and then heading back to campus. I was relieved that Eileen had seemed to enjoy herself and had asked me to stay at her dorm overnight so that I could really see what campus life was like. My parents thought it was a good idea, so I packed up for my first night on campus. I must say, it was the fun side of college that I hadn't experienced at my previous school. I met so many people and I laughed so much that I thought my cheeks would hurt for weeks. Then a huge unexpected lesson unfolded right in front of me.

I remember sitting at the top of the stairs in Eileen's dorm when her smile melted into a frown. I immediately thought that this would be the moment she decided she didn't like me or that I didn't fit in. I turned to her and instinctively began to apologize. I remember saying that I was so sorry for how loud and crazy my family was.

She quickly cut me off and said, "Vick, your family is not crazy. You have a *normal* family. You have the kind of family that I really didn't know existed." Tears slowly started to stream down her cheeks as she continued, "I thought that kind of family was only on TV. You are so lucky, my friend. You are so lucky."

Of course I was stunned because I had no idea what she was talking about. To me, my family was loud, crazy, and a bit embarrassing at times. She then turned to me and told me her life story—some of which was difficult to hear—and I quickly realized that my family wasn't so bad after all. Eileen's childhood was filled with a great deal of fear and pain. Her parents were plagued with addiction and were physically abusive to her and her six sisters. Eileen became the mama at a very young age. She felt it was her job to protect and take care of her sisters, because that's just who she is (or rather, who she learned to be). My dear friend also experienced sexual violence and never felt the love in her home that she had apparently felt at dinner with my family in that one evening.

After hours of talking, crying, and laughing, it was clear to me that I had made a forever friend. It also became apparent to me that not all childhoods were about riding bikes and playing in the sand. From that moment on, my eyes were wide open. I no longer saw childhood from just my own perspective. I was beginning to understand that this brief period of time was extremely different for each person; yet no matter what it looked like, it ultimately paved the road into adulthood. I now recognize that many of the struggles we face in adulthood can be alleviated by simply looking back at our childhood for guidance. The beliefs that we form as children are either helpful or detrimental. Either way, these are the ideas that we hold near and dear to our hearts. Their impact on our lives is often enormous.

Core Beliefs and the Garden of Life

As you read in the quote from *The Law of Attraction,* by Esther and Jerry Hicks, at the beginning of this chapter, a belief is a thought that you simply keep thinking. A core belief is a thought that begins in early childhood and is validated over time. Within the first five years of our lives, our core beliefs are set. These are born from thoughts that we have about ourselves or life in general and they dwell deep within our hearts (our core). We exit childhood with both positive and negative core beliefs. An empowering core belief might be *The Universe supports me and all is well.* A damaging core belief might be *I'm not worthy* or *I'm not enough.* These ideas are formed as we watch, listen to, and learn from our parents, caregivers, and teachers.

Core beliefs are like tiny seeds that are planted within your heart. When you plant a healthy seed and nourish it with unconditional love, it flourishes and expands to its full potential. Positive core beliefs begin here and provide you with powerful tools to handle life when it gets tough. It would be nice if all of the seeds that were planted in our garden of life were healthy, but unfortunately some of the seeds are toxic and can wreak a great deal of havoc. Because any seed will grow in a suitable environment, even toxic seeds will grow and flourish if nurtured. The more you think about and believe these thoughts (or seeds) to be true, the stronger they will become. All that negative core beliefs need to thrive are fearful thoughts. Unfortunately, most of us tend to focus more on the negative than the positive and this causes the harmful core beliefs to spread like weeds. Although I'm not an expert gardener, I do have good news for you about *your* garden of life: since a belief is a thought you keep thinking, when you choose to change your thoughts, you will also change your beliefs, and ultimately change your life! Stop watering the toxic seeds, and with time they'll stop growing—it's as simple as that.

A few years ago, I was teaching a unit on plants to my first graders. Each child was given a few seeds to plant in a clear plastic cup so that they could see what would happen to the seeds as they watered them daily and nourished them with sunlight. Every day the kids would enter the classroom with excitement and rush over to their plants to find out what was happening. They were delighted to see the roots sprouting downward in the cup and amazed by the growth of the plant above the soil each day.

One child came to me after a week or so with a look of concern and said, "Mrs. Savini, I think there's something wrong with one of my seeds."

I explained that it takes some seeds longer to grow than others and went to examine his cup. When I walked over to the cup I immediately noticed a hazy film growing around the seed, but didn't see any signs of roots or sprouts. It was just as interesting to me as it was to the children. Together we studied the specimen and made predictions and observations about what was happening.

Suddenly, one child blurted out, "I know. It's a bad seed!"

Another child quickly followed up with, "Yeah, it's a fungus—right, Mrs. Savini?"

I smiled at their use of vocabulary and encouraged them to journal their thoughts and predictions as we went on with our day.

Here I am, several years later referencing magical insights brought forth from my young and insightful students. Core beliefs are indeed seeds within our hearts. Some grow and flourish, adding love and light to our lives, while others act as a fungus or bacteria and bring about a great deal of pain and turmoil. Typically, we have many seeds planted in our gardens. Some give us the strength and stamina to get through difficult times, while others create those challenges we have to get through.

We all come out of childhood with a different combination of positive and negative core beliefs. Believe it or not, one of my greatest positive core beliefs was planted as a tiny seed by my fear-driven mother. In tough times, my mom always used to say, "God never gives you anything you can't handle," or "When God closes a door, He opens a window." These sayings came from her Christian upbringing and helped her when life presented challenges. I heard her say these things, but then saw her reacting to life with fear. This contradiction meant that her wisdom was lost on me for many years. Although it had been planted in my garden, I chose to pay more attention to the toxic seeds, for a few years anyway.

After a great deal of soul searching and use of the 7 Essentials (which I will share with you in Part II of this book), I can now access the true meaning of this positive core belief planted unknowingly by my mother many years ago. I personally don't believe that we are separate from God, and so my interpretation today of my mother's insight is slightly different, but nonetheless parallel. I was blessed with her seeds of wisdom and came to know that *the Universe is always bringing my highest good to me*. So when bad things happen, I opt for the popular saying, "This too shall pass," because I know in my heart that the Universe is guiding me to my highest good.

While we all possess positive core beliefs that give us strength, we also have toxic beliefs that, if allowed to, can spread like weeds in our garden and dim the light within. As you likely noticed from my opening story in this chapter, the negative core belief that has been a thorn in my side throughout my life is the belief that I am not enough. This is common for many of us because we've been taught that we are separate from God and we seek validation outside of ourselves. I've come to discover in working with clients in my coaching practice that most people have a primary negative core belief that they are not enough or not worthy. They then have at least one or two secondary beliefs that feed this primary core belief and cause issues in every aspect of their lives.

For years I've battled with this thought of not being enough, which has caused me to believe that I just don't fit in. The secondary beliefs that accompany this core belief have been: *I'm not smart enough, I'm not pretty enough,* and *I am not important.* I grew up in a poverty-thinking family where I often heard the words "We just can't afford that" or "We don't have enough." It was easy for me to assimilate this thinking into my everyday life and see myself as lacking as opposed to flourishing. This feeling of lack or un-worthiness spilled over into my relationships with friends, lovers, jobs, finances, and everyday life. I would say that my first graders summed up negative core beliefs quite well in saying that they're bad seeds or fungus.

The Birth of Core Beliefs

My mom was 34 years old when she gave birth to me. I was her fourth child, and I was born 11 years after my closest sibling. My eldest sister is 16 years older than I am (but she'll deny it if you ever ask), and my second-eldest sister is 15 years older than I am. My mom and dad got married very young: my mom was only 17 when they married; and she gave birth to my sister, Angela, just one year later. My sister Lucy was born when my mom was 19, and Sabrina was born when she was 23. Mom jokes that every time she went to the doctor with a cold, they told her she was pregnant. The last thing she expected when she went to the doctor not feel-ing well, 11 years after my sister Sabrina was born, was to hear, "Jeanette, you've got that same 'cold' again—you're pregnant." My parents were struggling to make ends meet financially with the three children they already had, so adding a fourth to the mix certainly put pressure on both of them.

Although my mom was excited to have another child, she was also a bit stunned by the news since she had thought she was done having babies. She got married young, had three children quite quickly, and had never really had time to find herself. It's clear now that she must have felt somewhat depressed and emotionally alone, because she was acting like a "human doing," spending all her time and energy taking care of the family. Her role—whether she liked it or not—was to take care of the kids and the home while my father provided for us. My two eldest sisters, being much older than I, thought it was fun to have a baby in the family because they could "mother" me as well. They would often take care of me and take me places to help my mother out. To this day, my sisters still call me "the baby," which raises the hairs on the back of my neck. My third eldest sister experienced being "the baby" for 11 years, until I came along, and as a result she felt a bit nudged to the side. Looking back, I now realize that I didn't have one mother—I had four! Throughout my life, all three of my sisters voiced their opinions, stepped in to protect me, and tried to guide me in one way or another. As a result, I never really learned to listen to my own thoughts and ideas because I had four strong women telling me what I *should* be thinking and doing.

I distinctly remember coming out of my bedroom one morning at the age of five with two different shoes on and asking which pair I should wear. My mother was there with two of my sisters and they all voiced their opinions. After they argued about it, they made the decision and told me which ones to wear. I didn't make many decisions on my own because I wasn't allowed to, and so I learned early on not to trust myself.

Do I, for one moment, think that any of them set out to hurt me? Absolutely not. Each one of these strong women tried to help me navigate the waters of life as best as they could. The issue is that they too were dealing with their own negative core beliefs and unknowingly immersing me in those as well. We all do this. We want to help our children or put them on the right path. However, the worst thing we can do is take their power away by making all of their decisions for them without asking them how they feel. My toxic seed is the belief that I am not worthy. But I'm proving that to be untrue as I work on changing my thoughts and applying the 7 Essentials to my daily life. You can do this as well!

Getting to the Root

When I'm working with a new client during a coaching session, our first order of business is uncovering negative core beliefs.

As I stated previously, I find that it's generally one primary belief and possibly a few secondary beliefs that feed the toxic seed and hold us back from being our absolute best. I firmly believe that it is important to uncover those core issues that are holding us back because we can't change the thought that is creating a belief until we know what it is that needs to be shifted.

My work with adults focuses on helping them nurture and provide for their inner child so that they are able to truly love themselves. Once we get talking, it's often easy for me to pinpoint the negative core belief that's holding them back, because it is threaded through all of their relationships and difficult life situations. In my work, I've found that there are actually only a few negative core beliefs that come up time and again. They include: *I'm not worthy, I'm not enough, I'm not competent, I'm not safe, I'm not important, I'm flawed.* When you boil these down, it's apparent that they all come from one source: lack of self-love. Isn't that what we're all dealing with? If I don't believe that I'm smart enough, then I don't truly love and accept myself. If I feel invisible, then I quickly determine that I'm not important and therefore, I'm unlovable. All negative core beliefs lead back to one root issue: lack of self-love. So the remedy, no matter what the negative core belief is, must be learning to love yourself. This is often easier said than done.

Some people are resistant to admit that their toxic seeds or negative core beliefs began in childhood, because they feel as though they had a good childhood and believe they couldn't possibly have learned so much negativity during that time. For years, I also felt guilty for feeling inadequate because, in my mind, I had no reason to feel this way. I was not physically or sexually abused. My parents loved each other and provided as best as they could for our family. They instilled strong moral values within each of us, and family was their number one priority. So who the hell did I think I was to have "issues"?

Many of my clients felt quite the same way when they first came to me. They felt that they needed some major traumatic event in their lives to justify feeling the way they were. But the truth is, you don't need major trauma in your childhood to carry core beliefs that can hold you back. Parents don't set out to harm their children on purpose. Yet many end up passing on baggage without realizing it, because they too have core beliefs that are holding them back.

If you think back to the twin daughter in Chapter 2, you might be able to pick out her negative or self-limiting core belief as *I'm flawed; there's something wrong with me*, which is ultimately the belief that she is not enough. This toxic seed came from a place a fear. There was a great deal of fear as she entered this world because of physical complications, and that continued into her early childhood. Her mom was fearful for her daughter's health, and so she unfortunately validated this belief without even realizing it. As the years went on, the little girl might continue to validate this belief on her own by comparing herself to others, including her twin sister, and feeling that she couldn't make decisions or do the things she wanted without help from others. But it doesn't have to be this way. The girl could choose self-love instead. She could learn to believe in herself by applying the 7 Essentials. By shifting her belief she would come to love and accept herself for the beautiful person that she truly is and therefore let her inner light shine.

In Chapter 2 you also read about Bella. Her core belief was that she was not important, and this began with her fear of abandonment. When you feel invisible or unimportant, you'll do just about anything to get attention. Perhaps Bella felt this way because she experienced the loss of a parent at a very early age. She felt a strong emotional dependency on her mom, which put pressure on their relationship. Bella also had a choice: she could continue to validate this belief and get caught up in other unhealthy relationships based on dependency, or she could learn the 7 Essentials which would help guide her back to her center or self-love.

There Is No Blame

Throughout my own childhood, I was very active in the arts. I was a dancer, a singer, an artist, and yes, even a writer! I had hardworking parents who taught us to be kind and generous and to always help others. I was praised for my successes. I was told how good and sometimes bad I was. As a result, I learned to depend on others for my self-esteem, self-image, and self-identity. I learned that I was not enough unless someone else told me that I was enough. Unfortunately, even when others told me I was good, I didn't believe it and I therefore didn't feel good enough. I was always looking for ways to be noticed and ultimately accepted. Because I received praise for the things that I did, I came to learn that gaining acceptance and approval from others was paramount. It wasn't who I was, but what I accomplished that mattered. All of these negative core beliefs stemmed from a lack of self-love. What no one ever taught me, as a child, was how to love myself.

While we all have some empowering core beliefs and some harmful ones, most of us tend to hold on to the harmful ones more permanently. If you're feeling stuck or a bit discouraged, I can guarantee you that there's a damaging core belief at the root of your feeling. A person who appears cold and callous is a person who believes that they're not loved or lovable. One who is angry and judgmental believes that they're not good enough. The people pleaser struggles to feel worthiness and can easily turn into an angry person. A know-it-all is someone who feels incompetent. A control freak feels that they aren't safe and therefore lacks trust in the Universe. The loud, obnoxious person who you turn from in disgust or the overachiever who always has to outdo everyone else was the child who felt invisible or unimportant. The next time you come across a person who rubs you the wrong way, I encourage you to imagine them as an infant with pure, innocent energy. Put yourself in their shoes for a moment and try to see the light within rather than the external layers they have accumulated as a result of self-limiting beliefs.

We always have two choices in life: love or fear. Fear will fertilize the toxic seeds, and love will allow our best selves to bloom. As adults, many of us have discovered our negative core beliefs, and we've had to peel back the layers from years of nourishing these toxic seeds in order to repair and strengthen our foundation. As parents, teachers, and caregivers, we can make a huge difference in the lives of our children by providing them with tools to look within and learn to love themselves at a young age.

As parents, we do the best we can with our children to nurture, love, and shape them, based upon our own backgrounds. Some experiences from our own childhoods were empowering and others were harmful; but we take the good with the bad and we parent our children to the best of our ability. As teachers, we do the same. There's never intent to harm the children who come to us for learning. That damage comes from the toxic seeds that are planted unconsciously. There is no need for blame, only awareness.

On any given day, I hear my name called about a hundred times. They come to me, their teacher, to show me their creations, to share their thoughts, and to seek my approval. What they really need to hear from me (and from their parents) is a simple comment that praises them, but more important, redirects them to look within and feel their own feelings about their idea, design, or accomplishment. Helping our children to see the light within means holding a mirror up to them and asking them to see, feel, and believe that they're important, whether the world acknowledges that or not.

Don't Shut Off the Light

One night while I was tucking my son into bed, I heard a subtle yet life-changing message. After giving my sweet boy a kiss and telling him I loved him very much, I turned to hit the light switch. He quickly blurted, "Mom, wait, whatever you do, don't shut my light off!" I looked at him as he was frantically arranging the nine million stuffed animals on his bed and smiled. In that moment something magical happened. For some reason his sweet, innocent plea not to turn the light off hit me like a ton of bricks. I realized that what our children need, more than anything else, is for us not to turn off their lights—not the physical lights in their bedrooms, but rather the lights that shine brightly within them from birth. They live in this magical, playful universe where all they want to do is grow, learn, and expand while having tons of fun. We adults, unfortunately, live in a parallel universe where we're dealing with self-limiting beliefs, trying to measure up and keep all of our balls in the air. We dim their lights so often without even realizing it, while unintentionally creating negative core beliefs.

Just a few hours prior to bedtime that night, I'd gotten upset with my son for giving up while reading with me. I barked at him for being lazy. In truth, he was likely just feeling frustrated because he'd had enough reading for the evening, but didn't want to let his teacher mom down. Does this make me a bad parent? No, it makes me a typical parent. It makes me a parent who is doing the best I can in every moment of the day, who sometimes gets caught up in fear or negative core beliefs. Luckily, I have the 7 Essentials to fall back on when fear starts creeping in, and by the end of this book, so will you.

Crossing the Bridge

Now that you've completed Part I, you hopefully have a better understanding of how our childhood dramatically impacts our lives and leads to the development of our core beliefs. At this point, you may be thinking about your own core beliefs—those that are holding you back and those that are helping you succeed. You may begin to wonder if you do, in fact, love yourself, or if that lack of self-love is making life harder than it needs to be. If you're searching for answers or validation outside of yourself, you're likely dimming your own light. You may be able to see that now.

And all those feelings you have about yourself are certainly being passed along to your children, consciously or unconsciously.

Well, remember this: you are whole, perfect, and complete just as you are. In *Saturday Night Live* character Stuart Smalley's words, "You're good enough. You're smart enough. And doggone it, people like you!" (And if they don't, tough shit—the only thing that matters is that you like yourself . . . or rather, that you love yourself.)

If we truly want to give our children a strong foundation and arm them with tools to navigate the waters of life, then we must embrace the light within. The first part of this book was dedicated to awareness—awareness that childhood is too precious to ignore because it is the foundation for the rest of our lives. Part II will present alternatives to all of those negative or toxic beliefs that you've held onto for years and that you unconsciously pass on to your children or the children you serve. That's right, I said it: "the children you serve." We are here for the children—those who walk the earth right now, and the children who live deep within our very own hearts.

IGNITE THE LIGHT:

The 7 Essentials

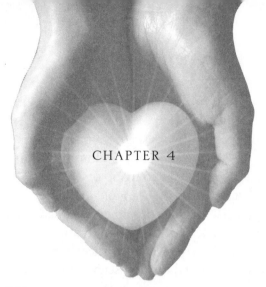

CHAPTER 4

ESSENTIAL #1:

Love Yourself

*"Love is the great miracle cure. Loving
ourselves works miracles in our lives."*

— LOUISE HAY

On September 11, 2011, I sat patiently in the audience at a
Hay House Movers & Shakers event in New York City. Movers &
Shakers is an event hosted by the publisher of this book, attended
by aspiring authors who are looking to learn how to publish an
empowerment book and connect with one of the largest empowerment publishing houses in the world. This was an interesting
morning because the energy in the city was tense and somber as
a result of it being the ten-year anniversary of the 9/11 tragedy.

Louise Hay stood up to speak at the start of the day. She obviously felt the same heavy energy we were all feeling, and she
moved to raise the vibration with her positive outlook and amazing, loving presence. After she addressed the audience, you could
see everyone's shoulders begin to relax and feel the mood in the

conference center shifting. Within the next hour, best-selling Hay House author Cheryl Richardson and Reid Tracy, Hay House's CEO, were going to bring a few people up to present their message or book idea. They were choosing randomly, but something deep inside me told me that I was going up on that stage.

The night before, we'd all been told to prepare a five- to seven-minute speech—just in case our name was called to go up onstage. Instead of going back to my hotel room and getting to work on the speech right away, I decided to meet my dear friend Eileen who lives close to the city. I hadn't seen her in years, and this was a perfect opportunity to reconnect. We went to dinner and spent quality time in the city, and then we were drawn to the 9/11 site. I felt as though I needed to be there. I just wanted to send lots of love and tons of light to help raise the vibration on this somber day. When I returned to my hotel room later that evening, I decided to put together my "just-in-case speech." I ended up staying up the whole night watching the inspirational movie *Bieber Fever* and preparing a speech that I would share, if given the opportunity.

As Cheryl and Reid began selecting people to join them up on the stage, I felt a lump begin to form in my throat, and I hesitated to raise my hand. Reid chose the first person, and I tensed up a bit. Cheryl chose the next person, and I could feel the fear rising as I struggled to get past my self-doubt and find the courage to raise my hand. I began to rehearse the speech I'd written in my head while trying to convince myself that I could do this. Finally, I bravely plunged my hand into the air just as Reid looked out into the audience in search of a third candidate. Our eyes met, and he pointed right at me.

My inner child was jumping up and down inside of me, while my ego began to pester me with thoughts of fear. I am not typically a person who writes speeches in advance because I like to let the words flow through me, but I had written a speech the night before in fear that I might be chosen and then freeze. As I walked toward the stage rehearsing the speech in my head, I heard a voice deep within say: *You're not talking about that today.* I felt panic begin to set in, yet I knew in my heart that I was being driven by something much bigger than myself. I took a deep breath, pushed fear aside, and began to speak my truth.

I still can't tell you exactly what I said that day—although most of it was probably what you're reading in this book—but I will tell you that one of the most powerful experiences in my life occurred at the very end of that speech. For some reason, as I was speaking I kept hearing the song, "The Greatest Love of All" by Whitney Houston playing in my head. Being a fly-by-the-seat-of-my-pants kind of girl, I decided to go with it, and I began to sing the words that expressed so many of my beliefs. As I reached the chorus, I looked out into the audience and heard everyone singing along with me—even Louise Hay! Chills ran down my spine. I could feel the vibration of everyone singing those beautiful words. It was the message of the song that united us that morning. It was the power of one—a deep understanding that somewhere in our hearts we were all connected. It was knowing (and believing!) that the greatest love of all is the love you have for yourself.

That Old Cliché

So what does that mean exactly, to love yourself? It sounds so clichéd to say, "Just love yourself!" It also sounds way too easy. Love can be defined in many different ways, but one of my favorite definitions is found on dictionary.com: "Love is a feeling of warm personal attachment or deep affection." Just reading that makes me feel all warm and fuzzy inside.

Now let's look at a few different examples of this feeling we call love. In the United States, we have a popular clothing store called Old Navy. Once a year, around the holidays, they come out with something they call Cozy Socks. These are made from the softest fiber I have ever felt. It's almost like walking on a cloud made of cotton balls. I usually don't like socks, but these are just so comfy that I can't help but love them. You see, in the middle of winter, when I come home from a long day at work and put on my Cozy Socks, I instantly feel comforted, relieved, safe, warm, accepted just as I am, and absolutely taken care of. I *love* my Cozy Socks! They give me a warm feeling every time I slide them on my tootsies.

On to example number two: My son read a book in school during the holiday season about a little boy who learns the true meaning of Christmas. In this story, the little boy realizes that it's not piles of toys that he really wants for Christmas, but rather a puppy he can love and who will love him back. My son came home that day, ran straight to our puppy, and gave him a great big hug. He said, "Beau Doodles, I love you so much. You mean so much to me. I will always take good care of you. I love you!" This is a great example of love. My son felt a warm personal attachment and was showing his deep affection for our dog.

The first example that I gave to define love was obviously an example of loving an inanimate object, but nonetheless, it gives you a perfect understanding of that warm personal attachment and deep affection. The other example was a more typical illustration of love. When you think about the love you feel for a friend, a relative, a lover, or a child, it certainly differs—but what remains the same is the way it makes you feel. I'm sure we can define this emotion in countless different ways, but the bottom line is that when you love someone or something, you like it a whole bunch! Now tell me, do you like yourself a whole bunch?

Think back to the Cozy Socks and answer these questions: Do you *comfort* yourself? Are you *relieved* to be you? Do you feel *safe* and warm within your own skin? Do you *accept* yourself just as you are? Most important, do you take *really good care* of yourself?

Giving our children a strong foundation begins with teaching them to love themselves unconditionally. Children cannot believe in themselves if they are not able to love themselves. The best way to teach our children self-love is to model a love for ourselves and give our children a daily practice of loving themselves. You will be given specific exercises that can be applied to the classroom or the home in Part III of this book, but try to stick with me as we explore the essentials needed to create strong foundations first.

Who Do You Love?

Of course we want our children to love and honor themselves. We wish for them to be able to see the beauty within so that they can grow and flourish. But do we teach them to love themselves by example, or do we preach self-love and hope that they get further along that road than we did?

My parents were always compassionate, loving people who felt that taking care of others was critically important. As I said earlier, my dad would take the shirt off of his back for another person if he felt that the other person needed it more. To this day, my mom is quite the same way. My parents' words taught us that you should always be kind, generous, loving, loyal, and genuine. These are admirable characteristics to pass on to your children; and I hope that I, in turn, have passed them on to my son. My parents' actions, on the other hand, taught us that you should always put the needs of others before your own and that it was selfish to look out for yourself. I watched as my parents were taken advantage of in many situations throughout my life. They always gave way more than they received. Sometimes they complained about it, but mostly they just continued with the same practice over and over again: always putting the needs of others before their own.

From watching my parents, my sisters and I learned to be caretakers. We learned that it was important to make others happy, and that if we could fix someone else's problems, then we would be validated for our efforts. As a result, we all grew up looking for approval from other people. We were never taught to look within or see ourselves as important. We had no idea that we were supposed to love ourselves. These early beliefs led to issues around codependency and resulted in many challenging relationships for me and my sisters. Codependency is defined as: "Excessive emotional or psychological reliance on a partner, typically one with an illness or addiction." You know—the people you think you can fix.

Did my parents realize that they were teaching us to be codependent? I certainly don't think so. Rather, they didn't know how to teach us to love ourselves, because they never truly learned how to love themselves. They only did what they thought to be right. They made themselves available to care for others and put their own needs last.

What I've come to learn in later life is that while it's wonderful to help others and even take care of them once in a while, this can't be done at the expense of your own well-being. What my parents modeled was giving so much that they drained themselves—mentally, emotionally, and sometimes even physically. We were taught that feeling drained was normal, and we weren't responding to life because we were desperately seeking approval. We learned to react to life and relationships with others instead of responding to them, because that was our core model.

When we react to life, we're usually driven by fear. We don't take time to think about what's happening and actually feel our feelings. Instead, we jump forward in a panic to quickly get through the situation. Perhaps we think we're problem solving, but in actuality we're putting a Band-Aid on the problem so that we can get through the pain quickly and make sure that everyone is content. When we respond to life, we take the time to feel the feelings and process the thoughts before taking action. We're generally driven by love in this state. There is a huge difference between reacting and responding to life. My parents didn't know this simple truth. I'm quite confident that they didn't set out to teach us how to be codependent, but since children are constantly learning from their parents, this was an unavoidable lesson in *our* curriculum of life.

What Matters Most Is How You See Yourself

When you look in the mirror, what do you see? Better yet, what do you feel? You may think a mirror is just for brushing your teeth, styling your hair, or examining your physical appearance, but the mirror can actually be a very powerful tool. Every summer I run a series of empowerment camps that aim to help kids believe in themselves and speak their truth. A friend of mine and I have been doing this for the past six years; and each year the camps get better, because we learn as we teach.

In 2012, we began teaching the 7 Essentials to the kids in our programs. It was during our Girls Rule Camp that we all felt something powerful happen. I was teaching the first essential in the list, Love Yourself, when the magic began. We were in a dance studio, and I asked all of the girls to line up in front of the mirror and look into their own eyes to recite positive affirmations. The girls ran to the mirror to jockey for a position, and we began with affirmations that I spoke aloud and they repeated. I then asked the girls to look into their own eyes and give themselves at least five compliments, using "I am..." at the beginning of each statement. Some examples were "I am kind. I am amazing. I am confident. I am friendly."

The girls had a few minutes to complete this task (which had many of them in fits of giggles), and then I stood in front of the mirror to demonstrate the final affirmation. I looked down the line of girls and then directly into my own eyes and said, "I am important." I was actually surprised by the conviction in my own voice and moved by the power in the room as the girls recited this affirmation with both confidence and strength. We repeated, "I am important" three times and then stared into the mirror for a moment of pure silence. I looked over at Stephanie, my co-director, and we both had tears in our eyes. It was evident that this moment was powerful as we all stood in awe, looking at ourselves in the mirror and feeling our importance.

We gave the girls a snack break so we could recoup and chat for a moment. We both knew something magical had just happened. We didn't need to say much, because we could both sense what was going on.

"Did you feel that?" I asked.

"I did. And so did all 37 girls!" Stephanie responded. She continued, tears streaming down her face, "No one ever told me that, Vick. No one told me that *I* had to think I was important. I thought I was important when others told me I was."

My eyes filled, because I was thinking the very same thing.

As a child, I learned that my self-esteem, self-image, and self-identity were all based on the thoughts and opinions of others. Now, as an adult teaching empowerment classes, I finally understood that what really mattered was how *I* felt about myself. To be able to look in the mirror and love the person staring back at you is so very important. And once you're able to do it for yourself, it will be much easier to show your children how it's done.

Morning Affirmation

Children learn from us whether we're aware of it or not. We are a continuous movie for them, streaming live, 24/7. They are essentially immersed in "our stuff" and creating their own "stuff" in the process of everyday life. All of this means that if you don't love yourself, it will be very hard for your children to love themselves. We can shower our children with affection and attention and spend all of our time doing everything we possibly can for them, but the truth is, you'll never teach a child to love him- or herself if you're not able to lead by example.

To help my students in the area of self-love, I include a morning ritual in my daily curriculum. Every day my students walk through the classroom door and begin their morning work. Shortly thereafter, I call them over to a central area that we call "the Meeting Place." Here, we conduct our morning meeting, through which I aim to set a positive tone for the day. First, we go through all of the typical classroom things like the calendar and the weather; then we move into something a little different. It's what I like to call "a lesson of the heart." We begin with positive affirmations. (An affirmation is quite simply anything you think, believe, and affirm to be true. Unfortunately, this means that you're likely creating negative affirmations daily, often without realizing it. But we will turn that around by the time you've completed this book.) By spring, the kids in my class will have gone through full "Savini training" and are pretty well versed in the power of affirmations and how to use them to turn negative thoughts around.

This part of the day is something that the kids look forward to. If I'm rushing through the morning meeting for some reason, they never let me forget that we need to choose an affirmation for the day. I use a beautiful kid-friendly card deck from www.magnif icentcreations.com. Each morning, one child is chosen to pick the affirmation randomly from the deck. That child reads the affirmation to the group, and we all repeat it together. We then discuss what it means to us before pinning it up on our white board to review throughout the day. If you truly want an affirmation to work, you can't just say it once and expect a magic genie to make it a reality. Rather, you must focus on that affirmation throughout the day, repeating it over and over again until it becomes your truth.

I still remember one spring morning when the affirmation chosen by one of my students was *I am important.* I smiled when I saw this one come up and turned to the children to ask what it meant to them. Several children raised their hands eager to share their thoughts. They said things like, "It's okay to be me. I am special. I am good at being a kid. I matter." Then my little friend Bella raised her hand and said, "Mrs. Savini, I am important means that we are all perfect just the way we are!" Now, if you remember the story about Bella from Chapter 2, then you'll understand the depth of that statement. (Bella is the little girl who was acting out to get attention and showing no remorse.)

I was so proud of my students in that moment, because as Bella said those words, they all nodded their heads in agreement. In that instant I knew that being a good teacher wasn't about an APPR (annual professional performance review) or how well students do on tests. It was about helping kids learn to value and love themselves the way they are. This was the most important gift I could give my students. I knew that I was effective because my kids clearly demonstrated that they were learning to love themselves.

I often recommend that my adult clients use affirmation cards as well. If you were to hold my iPhone in your hand, you'd quickly find a folder titled "Inspiration." Open that folder, and you'd see all of my affirmation apps, angel cards, and meditations. I, too, use these daily affirmations to raise my vibration! If you're interested in some of the apps that I personally use, simply go to Oceanhouse Media. There you will find some of the best inspirational apps to inspire and reconnect you to your inner light. (We'll talk more about adult affirmations in Chapter 12.)

Love yourself is the first essential to being our best self because our toxic seeds cannot grow and flourish if we have a *warm personal attachment to, or deep affection for,* the person staring back at us in the mirror. You may see that the remaining six essentials sequentially lead us back to self-love. That's simply because, to paraphrase Whitney Houston, learning to love ourselves is truly the greatest love of all.

CHAPTER 5

ESSENTIAL #2:

Feel Your Feelings

"The best and most beautiful things in the world cannot be seen or even touched. They must be felt with the heart."

— HELEN KELLER

Are you in touch with your feelings? I mean are you aware of when you are feeling happy, sad, annoyed, depressed, angry, nervous, or excited? Perhaps the more important question is, do you *allow* your feelings to *guide* you, or do you avoid the uncomfortable feelings and rush them away as soon as they come up?

Several years ago I learned that my feelings were, in fact, guiding me in all the decisions I made. I picked up a book by Esther and Jerry Hicks entitled *Ask and It Is Given,* hoping that I would learn how to manifest my desires. I did learn how to do that, but more important, I learned the significance of feelings and emotions. You see, it's so easy to get caught up in what we're *doing* that we forget to honor how we're *feeling.* Remember, we are human *beings* not human *doings.* We all experience tons of different feelings within each day; yet many of us repress these emotions because we don't have time to address them, we don't want to deal with them, or we don't know how to handle them. We're often so focused on wanting peace and happiness that we try to get rid of the painful feelings as quickly as possible. We have been trained to believe that pain, sadness, or discontentment of any kind is bad.

What I've learned is that this is not actually the case. Emotions are a natural indicator of what's safe or right for us and what isn't safe or is veering from our truth. Esther and Jerry Hicks teach us that our feelings are indicators or guidance to finding the truth within. Most of us weren't taught to see our feelings this way, as an "emotional guidance system." Rather than using them to let us know when we're connected to the light within and when we're not, we tend to ignore or bury all the "bad" feelings and seek out only the "good." As a result, we tuck away our negative emotions—which should actually be serving as red flags—in the hopes that they'll disappear or be forgotten. In reality, they never actually disappear, and we're rarely able to forget about them. Instead, they lie dormant like an inactive volcano, bubbling and waiting to erupt.

It's as if we have a drawer within ourselves, and when something comes up that we don't like, we do our best to shove it inside and slam the drawer shut. The problem is, this drawer resides deep within our hearts. So when we stuff away our negative feelings, they take up all kinds of space and leave little room for the feelings we really do want to feel. If there's no room left in the drawer, then we limit the space available for us to feel joy, love, and acceptance. In other words, if we aren't feeling *all* of our feelings—the bad, the good, and the ugly—in the present moment, then we stuff them deeper. When they arise again, we may have a tendency to numb them or disconnect in order to function. This leaves us feeling empty, alone, and detached from the world and has led many individuals down the road of addiction or codependence in adulthood. Ignoring or "stuffing" our emotions can lead to many issues, including feelings of isolation or depression and unstable relationships. However, as I see it, the most critical concern is that when we ignore our feelings we turn off our "emotional guidance system," and we disconnect from the light within.

If you're ignoring or stifling your feelings like this, then chances are it's something you learned to do at a very young age (whether you realize it at first or not). And if you're always shutting down your own feelings, then you're most likely teaching by example, passing to the children in your life the very same habits and practices you formed at a young age. This perpetuates the cycle of stuffed emotions.

In the summer of 2012, the importance of "feeling your feelings" was magnified for me when I listened to the words of an 11-year-old who was expressing the pain she felt as a result of holding in her true emotions. It was the first time I'd ever presented the 7 Essentials to a group of children. We were all sitting in a circle at one of our summer camps, and when I got to the second Essential that I speak of here, one of the young girls put her head down and began to cry. I went to her side, put my arm around her, and asked what she was feeling. She took a while to respond and finally said, "Sad. I feel sad because you're telling us to feel our feelings, but when I feel my feelings my parents tell me to get over it or stop being so dramatic!"

As I glanced around the room, what I saw spoke volumes. All of the girls were nodding their heads in agreement. My intent with this Essential was to teach the girls that it was absolutely necessary to honor their feelings instead of ignoring them, because those feelings served as clues to what was right or wrong for them. Somehow I'd forgotten that the critical issue that needed to be addressed was how our feelings were being shut down in the first place. In this case, it was obvious that the young girl's feelings were being dismissed because she was being told to stop being so dramatic when she tried to express her sadness or disappointment. In other words, she was indirectly being told to stuff her feelings in that drawer and slam it shut. We spent nearly an hour discussing the importance of feeling our feelings, learning to trust our inner guidance system, and also learning how to deal with others who are telling us to shut off or stuff away our feelings.

As we talked, I was taken back to my own childhood and I began to remember how I, too, had been taught to repress and ignore my feelings.

I'm Moving Out!

When I was young, my family had an annual Memorial Day barbecue to celebrate the holiday, as well as both of my parents' birthdays, which were right around the same time. When I was in first grade, something happened that I can now identify as one of the first times I remember being taught to repress my feelings. The kitchen was full of chaos as my mom prepared for the day. As usual, my sisters were doing their own thing while the rest of the family was involved in preparing for the celebration. I distinctly remember being quite excited about a picture that I'd drawn and wanting desperately to share it with someone (for validation, of course). Each person I went to just kind of blew me off or said something like, "Oh yeah, that's nice, Vicki."

No one seemed to care about the cute kid with curls who had a beautiful creation in hand and wanted to share it. They were all too busy. Although there were tons of people at my house—my sisters, parents, aunts, uncles, and cousins—I felt completely alone and totally invisible. This wasn't the first time I'd felt this way. I tried to talk to my mom about it, but she just said, "Just go find something to do until the kids get here." I went to one of my sisters with tears in my eyes and said, "Nobody cares about me." Her response: "Stop being such a baby!"

I remember going off to my bedroom and writing a poem about how I felt. But that didn't alleviate the darkness in my heart—I wanted to be noticed. I wanted to be seen, and I wanted to know that I was important. This was all long before I understood the importance of loving myself. After sitting in my room for a while, I got the idea that if no one really cared where I was, then I would pack my bags and head on out. Yes, a bold seven-year-old I was (my son totally takes after me in that respect).

I packed my pajamas, a few outfits, and two stuffed animals in my Hello Kitty suitcase. Then I proceeded to strut through the busy kitchen with my bag and stuffed bunny in hand. I grabbed a few snacks for the road and announced loudly that I was leaving. My mom was at the sink and she turned just slightly to ask where I was going.

My response was curt: "Where I'm wanted!"

Mom turned back toward the sink and giggled before saying: "Well, don't forget your toothbrush and jacket. It might get cold later."

I was hurt by her insensitive response and annoyed that she found all of this so funny. I stomped out of the kitchen without my toothbrush or my jacket. I went through the back door, shaking my head because I couldn't believe that she really didn't care that her youngest child was running away. I was sick of being told to go entertain myself or to stop being such a "baby" when something was bothering me.

My dad was in the backyard cleaning the grill. I was certain that he would show compassion and stop me from leaving.

I gave him a hug and a kiss and said, "I'm leaving."

He turned to me, looked down at my suitcase, and replied, "Before dinner? You might want to eat first."

He, too, seemed to think this was funny. My heart sank because I was now starting to really believe that my family didn't care about me. I had seriously believed that if they saw me with my suitcase, they'd realize that they'd been ignoring me and start paying attention. No such luck. I took my suitcase and my stuffed bunny and headed down the driveway.

When I got to the front porch of our house, I realized that my plan hadn't worked. I just wanted my family to notice me—to see me—but they hadn't. Worst of all, no one appeared to care that I was actually leaving. Instead, they found it funny and obviously weren't taking me seriously. I set up camp on the front porch. I sat there for what seemed like an eternity (but was likely only about 15 minutes).

First I felt angry and annoyed; I soon shifted back to my original feelings of sadness and loneliness. I pulled my knees to my chest, buried my head, and hugged my legs for comfort. I let it all out, sobbing uncontrollably. No sooner had my first tear hit the porch than I felt my dad's enormous hand gently grasping my shoulder. He sat next to me and put his strong arm around me in a hug. I sobbed and sobbed as he held me.

Finally, he said, "You know, I'd be really sad if you ran away."

I lifted my head and hugged him. I wanted to blurt out a thousand things about feeling invisible, and unwanted, and ignored, but in that moment none of it mattered.

My dad smiled and asked, "What's going on, honey?"

I told him that I felt like no one cared about me because no one ever wanted to really listen to me. Before I could finish he quickly jumped in (as most parents would, in an attempt to stop their child from feeling pain) and said, "That's not true! Everyone loves you!"

As the words came off of his lips I felt my blood begin to boil once more. Now I really felt invisible because he was telling me that I shouldn't be feeling how I was feeling. He was telling me that my feelings were unfounded and untrue. Meaning, I must be making it up.

He clearly noticed the look of disgust on my face because he changed his tune and said, "I'm sorry you feel that way. Is there anything I can do?"

I smiled and said, "Yes, can I show you my picture?"

Dad smiled back, grabbed my suitcase, and together we headed into the yard. I could hear my sister snicker as we walked by: "Little brat got her way again." That hurt. But, looking back, I now realize that she was just *reacting* to the situation because she, too, had learned to suppress her true feelings.

As I retell this story, I can recall several other times during my childhood when I was told to toughen up, get a thicker skin, shake it off, or stop being so dramatic. We have all done this to our children. In fact, I have even caught myself saying these very same words to my own child and to children in my classroom.

The difference is that I now stop the moment I catch myself. Instead of telling them to "suck it up," I physically get down on the child's level to ask them what they are feeling. Then I pay close attention to their response and help them get through the feeling, promising them that it's okay to have these negative emotions because they ultimately teach us to trust ourselves.

After writing this particular section of the book, I read it to my mom and then listened as she shared her perspective. All these years later, she was still laughing about that morning. I can see why she was laughing now, but as a child I could not. Apparently my dad had packed his bags several times as a young boy, but hadn't gotten far either. When I heard her tell his story, I actually felt a bit sad for him because I knew that had been my dad's cry for help. My father had always felt invisible as a child because he had a twin brother who was favored by their mother. I immediately connected with his pain as my mom explained to me how similar we had been. My mom also gained some insight into how I'd been feeling as a child. She never really thought that she was stuffing away my feelings or encouraging me not to feel them. But in hindsight she realized that's exactly what had been happening. She also asked me to mention here that I was never out of their sight, because she'd been watching me through the front window on the porch, which is likely why my dad came to the rescue so quickly. (There you go, Mom. I love ya!)

The Light Inside of Me

Several years ago, I walked into my school in August to begin preparing for a new year. As I turned to walk down the hallway toward my classroom, I noticed that the entrance had been boarded up. I walked to the front desk to ask what was going on. To my surprise, half of our school had been closed because they'd found asbestos. We were required to team up with other teachers whose rooms were in the opposite end of the building until the asbestos had been removed safely. As a result, I had the opportunity to collaborate with a friend and fellow teacher that year. It was an amazing year for so many reasons, but the most unforgettable was the birth of *The Light Inside of Me.*

I had 18 students that year, and my teaching partner had 17. Both groups were crammed into one classroom. There were certainly pros and cons to this setup. My partner had a little boy named Billy in her class who was very angry. He would get annoyed and lash out at her or the other kids for seemingly no reason at all. I knew there had to be more to his anger. The great thing about co-teaching is that while one teacher is teaching a lesson, the other can prepare for the next lesson, or work with a small group of students who require more attention. With two teachers, you really learn more about the kids, because you've got two sets of eyes and ears on them.

One day my partner was teaching a writing lesson in the front of the classroom, and Billy was just not cooperating. He was mimicking her and talking back. Instead of reprimanding him, I walked over to the computer on the other side of the room and began typing out a poem. I had been using poetry as a way of coping since I was seven, so this was second nature to me. I recognized that he was mimicking the teacher because he wanted to draw attention away from the fact that he was feeling inadequate. I wanted to help him process those feelings. So I sat down and wrote this poem. It just poured out of me.

The Light Inside of Me

Deep inside me is a light,
that burns and glows and shines so bright.
To make my light shine bright—
I make good choices and do what's right.
My light shines brightest when I am kind,
and when I take time to just unwind.
When my light is dim—
I know it's time to look within.
My light is dim when I'm angry, sad, or mean,

and sometimes, when I feel unseen.
Deep inside me is a light,
that burns and glows and shines so bright.
I shine my light for all to see—
by making good choices for you and me!

I quickly printed a copy for each child with a basic writing prompt that said, "My light is brightest when . . ." As soon as it was my turn to step in and begin teaching, I introduced the lesson while looking right at Billy. That lesson opened him up in ways I could never have imagined. We began to see where his anger was coming from and were able to give him tools to express his feelings in a healthy way.

I love that poem because it was written in about ten minutes for little Billy but has inspired and empowered countless children. Even more important is that I didn't question the words coming through me. I simply went with the feelings I had as I sat at the computer and typed. It just *felt* right. This is what can happen when you don't ignore your feelings! That poem hung on the wall behind my desk for at least three years until I finally realized that it was meant to be a children's book. And that's exactly what it became in May 2010 (www.thelightinsideofme.com).

If you look at the words in the poem, you promptly see why it's important for kids to feel their feelings. Their feelings let them know what's good and what's not. It's a simple concept with a huge impact. Feeling your feelings means honoring the light within. Kids quickly learn that when they make a bad choice or when something isn't right, they can feel it in their hearts. And when they make good choices, it feels right and they feel like they're beaming from within. This has helped me not only teach kindness and responsibility to children but also help them to honor their feelings and keep themselves out of danger.

Feelings Are Real and Meaningful

I spent a few months working with a seven-year-old girl named Amanda whose parents were concerned because she wouldn't go to sleep unless one of them was with her. She had somehow developed a fear of her parents leaving, and none of them were sure where it was coming from. These were good parents with strong values who would never leave their children alone—especially at night. I knew there must have been an event that led to this behavior. I saw it as my job to dig a bit deeper to determine what was causing the fear for Amanda.

We had only met a few times when the incident that was causing her fear came up in discussion. Amanda is the eldest daughter of three, so she'd learned to be a "helper" and felt a certain level of responsibility for her siblings. On one particular day, the sisters were at the neighborhood library with their mom when the two younger girls needed to use the bathroom. Because Amanda didn't have to go, her mom had allowed her to stay where she was and continue reading her book. The library was in a safe location and was filled with neighbors and friends from their tight-knit community, so the mother felt that Amanda would be safe for a few minutes on her own. Unfortunately, while her mom was in the bathroom with the girls, a stranger tried to talk to Amanda. She immediately tensed up and didn't speak a word. She couldn't even recall what the man had said to her, but she knew that she *felt* unsafe. Her mom returned from the bathroom within minutes, and Amanda looked a bit shaken, but she only spoke briefly about the incident. Her mom assured her that she was now safe, and they left the library without talking further about what had happened.

As soon as this came up in our session, I knew this was the event that was causing her fear. For all we know, this could have been a very nice man just making conversation because he saw that her mom had left for a moment and didn't want the child to feel lonely. But you never know, and this is another reason why children need to honor their feelings—no matter what. Amanda and I talked with her mother about this incident, and her mom felt awful that she hadn't discussed it in greater detail with her daughter. But truthfully, she said, it didn't seem to be a real issue at the time. She asked Amanda if she was okay and gave her a hug, and they left the library. Unfortunately, Amanda said she was okay, but she really wasn't. When the mother thought back on that day, she remembered noticing that Amanda was very quiet, but the day got away from her and then more time passed.

The most important lesson here is that Amanda's feelings were real and meaningful, but she chose to stuff those feelings because she believed that they were unimportant. She certainly had a strong feeling, but chose to push it down so that she didn't have to deal with her fear. Ultimately, that incident created anxiety within her that she wasn't safe; and whenever her parents weren't right by her side (like at bedtime), she felt insecure. It was important for Amanda to learn that honoring her feelings and talking about them would give her power and help her to feel safe. We worked together on allowing her feelings to come up and sharing them with a trusted adult. It was critical that Amanda understood that when she felt fear or nervousness, it was important to talk about that with her trusted adult instead of ignoring the feeling and pushing it away. Our work together helped her to understand that it was necessary to feel her feelings and talk about them so that she felt safer. This ultimately taught her to honor her feelings—or as some would say—trust her gut. This simple understanding gave Amanda her power back.

It is critically important that we teach our children that it's not only acceptable to feel their feelings, but *necessary*—because this is how we learn to trust ourselves and listen to the voice within. You cannot truly love yourself if you don't trust yourself. As parents and teachers, we're not teaching our children to stuff their feelings intentionally. When a child cries or whines or even complains, it taps a nerve within us, and we often find ourselves in the same predicament as when our own feelings bubble up. We either don't have time to address these feelings, we don't want to deal with them, or we simply don't know how to handle them.

Instead of shutting down children (or yourself) when feelings come up, hit the pause button and ask how this feeling is guiding you. It may be leading you away from a bad choice or helping you to make a very hard decision, or it just might be your spirit calling your attention to something important. Whatever the guidance, feelings are important because they teach you to rely on yourself, and a huge part of loving yourself and shining your inner light is learning to listen to the voice within by trusting your feelings.

Despair, depression, and "dis-ease" in the human body are what come from a life of stuffing your feelings. When our feelings come up and we push them down or try to ignore them, they find a place to settle—often deep within our hearts. Over time, these repressed feelings weigh heavy on our minds and hearts, and they begin to deplete either our physical or emotional health. We often become immobilized or "stuck," and we're certainly no good to children when we're in this state.

Not allowing your feelings to fully process is like putting up a wall around your heart. You limit the capacity to feel and it becomes difficult for you to truly love others because the wall around your heart creates an obstacle for loving yourself. When you do not love yourself, you cannot love others because you don't see yourself as worthy of love, and you don't truly understand a deep feeling of love.

Allowing our children to feel their feelings means giving them the opportunity to experience the highs and lows and process them fully, instead of stuffing them away and hoping that they'll just disappear. While this can be difficult for parents because no one wants to see their children suffer, it's necessary in order to teach them how to trust and listen to themselves. Teachers also play a huge role in helping kids experience their emotions and feelings. Children spend several hours a day with their teachers, building upon their foundation. Kids need this Essential as part of their foundation in order to navigate the waters of life successfully as they grow up. And we adults need this key practice in order to be fully present with the children in our lives. When we're in touch with our feelings, we have a clear connection to the light within.

If you can relate to that "drawer" I've described in this chapter, then perhaps it's time to clean it out—feel your feelings and make room to be fully present in your life and the lives of others. I promise you won't regret it!

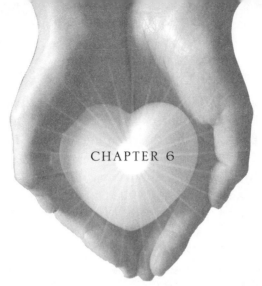

CHAPTER 6

ESSENTIAL #3:

Quiet the Mind

"Quiet the mind and the soul will speak."

— MA JAYA SATI BHAGAVATI

Are you mindful or is your mind full? How often do you catch yourself stuck in your own thoughts? Perhaps you feel like you're on a hamster wheel—always thinking and running from one experience to the next. Maybe you have so much on your mind that you feel the need to constantly make lists because your thoughts give you the feeling that you're spinning or off-balance. The act of making lists in and of itself is not the problem; the problem occurs when the list never ends! If your mind is racing with thoughts, then you'll always find more to do and will remain disconnected from the present moment. You are therefore not mindful but rather mind full.

I pride myself on being mindful and have actually been labeled "The Mindful Teacher," but we *all* have our moments. One night while I was rushing to prepare dinner for my family before getting my son off to soccer practice, I had a distinct moment of clarity. I had a billion thoughts racing through my mind as I took my son's fish sticks out of the oven and asked, "Honey, do you want to dip these in ranch dressing or ketchup?"

He quickly responded, "Mom, come on, don't you know me?"

I stopped in my tracks and welled up with tears because in the not-so-distant past, my son would never have had to ask me that question. I *know* in my heart that my son's choice is always ranch dressing with his fish sticks. That's all I needed to re-center myself and reconnect to the present moment because it was clear to me that I was not being mindful.

Sadly, I'd been so distracted by my thoughts—about my daily responsibilities, concerns about where things are heading in education, writing this book, and other pressing issues—I'd completely disconnected from the present moment. My mind was filled with random and insignificant thoughts, spinning like that hamster wheel. And while it was painful to see the look on my son's face when he thought for a second that I'd forgotten who he was and what his preferences were, there was a beautiful lesson in this moment for me. I was going through the actions of my daily life on autopilot—I'd allowed myself to become a human *doing* instead of a human *being*. I'm truly thankful that my son's simple, sarcastic response brought me back to the present and allowed me to recognize just how easy it is to fall into the trap of succumbing to the spinning wheel of thoughts.

So what is it that's on our minds all the time? Finances, family issues, career, colleagues, relationships, responsibilities . . . the list goes on. Most of us spend a great deal of time in our heads, planning what we have to do or want to do and how we'll go about doing it. In all of this planning and doing, we aren't *being*. And if we aren't being, then we're not in the present moment and certainly not mindful.

There are several definitions for mindfulness, but there's one I found that is simple and right to the point (just the way I like it). In their 1999 article "Mindfulness and Meditation," clinical psychologists G. Alan Marlatt and Jean L. Kristeller defined mindfulness as "bringing one's complete attention to the present experience on a moment to moment basis." I like this definition because when we aren't focused on the present moment, we're missing the gift that's right in front of us—the present.

I believe most of us spend too much time rehashing the past and forecasting the future. When we live in the past, we're giving ourselves permission to feel stuck and are adding layers of validation to those toxic seeds that dwell deep within our hearts. When we forecast the future, we're typically trying to prevent those negative core beliefs from expanding in our hearts. Both scenarios create fear-driven thoughts and dim the light within, making it more difficult to reveal our very best selves. It's easy to allow the mind to travel back in time or fast-forward to the future when we're stuck in our thoughts. When we're not living in the present moment, it's easy to become a human *doing*—focusing all of our attention on what we have done, what we haven't done, or what we think we must do. When we're stuck in our thoughts like this, we're not truly living. Instead, we merely exist.

So I ask you again: are you mindful? In other words, are you chained to your past, planning too much for the future, or living in the present moment as often as possible? If you were able to relate to the "human doing" description above, then chances are you're "existing" through life, rather than living it. That, my friend, is like sleepwalking—you're missing all of the good stuff!

Mindfulness in Motion

We all tend to do a little bit of sleepwalking through life, but my son has been a magnet that pulls me back to the present moment whenever I go astray. One day we were driving down a country road as we headed to a birthday party in my hometown. Our journey was going to take us about 90 minutes, and as we drove, my mind began to fill with random thoughts and concerns. Nico was playing his DS in the back seat while I was trying my hardest to clear my *full* mind. We were only about 20 minutes into our drive, and I was already feeling the stress beginning to overwhelm me. I found myself shifting from thoughts about my career to how long the drive would take and what I could be doing with the time instead.

As we traveled, I noticed a dog near the side of the road. He was an adorable hound dog, and he looked like he had a tag around his neck, signifying that he certainly had an owner. I saw that he was dangerously close to the edge of the winding road, so I beeped my horn as I saw a few cars approaching in the opposite direction. This piqued the dog's attention and thankfully caused the cars to slow down, avoiding what could have been a terrible incident. I continued to drive slowly, thinking about that poor dog and wondering if his owner even knew he was outside. I got back into the flow of traffic and started to pick up speed. Of course my random thoughts once again started to roll in. Now added to the mix were thoughts of guilt for not stopping to be sure that the dog was home with its owner.

Soon we were about two miles away from the dog, and I was still feeling bad about the little guy. I was also focusing on where we had to go—not at all mindful of the present moment. I looked in the rearview mirror, and my son had tears in his eyes. I asked him what was wrong and he quickly replied, "Mom, we have to go back to make sure that dog is okay. We just have to!"

I paused for a moment and then turned the car around to go find that dog, hoping and praying that he was okay. As we approached the spot where we first saw him near the road, we noticed that he was heading toward a house with people who appeared to be his owners. I pulled into the driveway and talked to them for a few minutes. It turns out that our beeping had drawn their attention outside and made them realize that the dog was loose. They were very thankful, and we were delighted that we had made a difference by being mindful.

As we started back out on the road I recognized a feeling in my heart of pure bliss. I looked in the mirror toward my son and said, "Nico, I am so proud of you for asking Mommy to go back to make sure that dog was okay. You are such a kind and caring young man, and you did the right thing." I smiled and continued on with tears in my eyes.

A few minutes later, I looked in the mirror again and saw my son wiping tears from his eyes. I asked what was wrong once again and he replied, "Nothing, Mommy, these are just tears of joy."

Up until the moment when we saw the hound dog on the side of the road, I had been caught up in my own "stinkin' thinkin'" yet again. I was thinking of all the things I needed to do and how long this trip was going to take. I was focusing on what was to come and what had already happened rather than what was right in front of me. You would think that just seeing the dog almost lose his life would have been enough to break the cycle of my thoughts—but it wasn't. Once the dog was out of sight, my mind began to race again, and it wasn't until my son— a six year old— forced me to be in the moment that I actually came back to the present. He hadn't even questioned going back to check on the dog. If he had been driving that car, he likely would have pulled over as soon as he saw the dog near the edge of the road. His first and only thought was to be sure that dog was safe. He was so clearly present in that moment, not at all caught up in thoughts about where we had to be or what lay ahead on the road to get there.

When we first began our journey that day, I'd felt a bit heavy in my heart. I'd wanted to raise my vibration but wasn't sure how. I considered playing one of the empowerment CDs I had in my car, but I wasn't convinced that would do the trick. My mind was just too full. It wasn't until I shifted my thoughts away from the future and into the present that my spirits lifted and I felt the light within ignite.

When moments like this occur, I always feel blessed to have simple reminders that help me to stay in the present moment. In the grand scheme of things, it really didn't matter that we were a few minutes late for the birthday party. I certainly wouldn't have solved my day-to-day concerns during that car trip, nor would I have solved the problems of the world. Staying in the moment can bring about so many blessings. I was blessed that my son was mindful enough to bring me back into the present. I often find that the children in my life teach me such great lessons. But, even kids are subject to "busy minds" these days. With mounting pressure, it's becoming harder for them to stay present as well.

Our Noisy World

Our kids are growing up in a world of constant noise. They're downloading music at the ripe old age of five. They play Angry Birds and Minecraft with the volume on full blast until their little fingers can't move anymore or the battery in their device of choice needs a charge. They sit in front of the television, mesmerized for hours, and most feel the need to make some sort of noise if they happen to find themselves in a moment of silence. Some kids hum, some make clicking noises, and some talk incessantly to fill the void of quietness. As parents and educators, we often stamp our children with some sort of label to explain why they have all of this energy. We spend hours trying to come up with ways to settle them down. Yet what we're not doing is teaching them how to unplug from the electronics and the noise in their heads and to plug into the light within themselves. Most of us don't know how to quiet our own minds, so how can we possibly teach our children? Imagine how different life would be if you'd been given that skill at a young age. How would life look if you were comfortable in silence and knew how to shut out the noise?

Shutting It Down

Shut off the television, put away the smartphone, and move away from the computer. You can't really love yourself or trust your inner voice when there is a constant racket in your head. Once you've removed the obviously distracting things, it's time to take care of the noise in your mind—the continuous thoughts and mental to-do lists.

Sit in a quiet, comfortable space, and allow yourself to just breathe in through your nose slowly and mindfully. Then release your breath through your mouth gently and calmly. Relax your body into a cozy chair or a spot on the floor, the bed, or the couch. Put one hand on your heart and one on your belly. Again, breathe in through your nose, with your eyes closed, and out through your mouth. Repeat this process over and over again until you feel your heart rate slow down, your body completely relax, and your mind surrender. If a thought comes into your mind, simply welcome the thought with the in breath, and then release the thought with the out breath. Each time, return your focus to the sound of your breath. Imagine a bright white light spinning gently just above the top of your head. Envision this light tenderly and gradually moving over your face, down your throat, and into your heart center. As you imagine the light passing parts of your physical body, continue to breathe deeply in through your nose and out through your mouth. Feel the warmth from the white light as it passes down over your entire body and grounds you to the earth. Feel the safety of this loving light that surrounds and embraces you. Breathe deeply—in through the nose and then out through the mouth—listening to your very own breath, feeling your very own heart gently beating to its own rhythm. Stay in this place of calm and silence for a little while because you deserve it! Your mind is now quiet and peaceful, and all is well.

Now that I have your full attention, let's talk about the importance of teaching our children to quiet their minds.

I'm Medicating!

I teach in the public school system, and for many years I have taught my students the same lesson you just learned in the preceding section. But it wasn't because I instinctively knew how to teach it. Rather, I was guided by the children in my class. You see, several years ago—around the time that the remake of the movie

Freaky Friday with Jamie Lee Curtis and Lindsay Lohan came out in theaters—my first grade students came back into the classroom after lunch and recess, and they were exploding with energy. I needed to round them up and get started with teaching, so after five minutes of chaos I said, "Okay ladies and gentlemen, let's go over to the Meeting Place to take some deep breaths!" The children began to file over to the rug where we met daily for our Morning Meeting and Community Meetings throughout the day.

When all the children were seated, I took my seat and noticed one child sitting cross-legged with his elbows on his knees and his hands in the air. His thumbs and index fingers were gently touching and his eyes were closed. I took one look at him and asked, "Alex, what are you doing?"

He opened one eye while squeezing the other tightly shut and said, "I'm medicating!" (Yes, you read that correctly, he said medicating, not meditating.)

I chuckled and replied, "Alex, honey, it's called meditating—and what a great idea!"

I then had the entire group of students do exactly what I had you do just a moment ago—mindfully breathe. That was several years ago, and this practice has become a constant in my classroom ever since. Thank you, Alex!

The Voices of Fear and Love

Deep inside each and every one of us is a voice that we listen to that helps us make decisions and guides us through life. This voice is divided by love and fear. Many of us spend the majority of our time listening to the voice of fear—all of those downloads that we've taken in over the years that add layer upon layer to our toxic core beliefs. The voice of fear can be quite loud and is usually difficult to ignore. We often find ourselves caught up in the moment and interested in what this voice has to say, even though we know in our hearts it doesn't *feel* right. It's comparable to watching the news as a tragedy unfolds in front of us. It frightens us or perhaps turns our stomach to watch or listen to the reporting, but we're drawn in because we can't believe this is actually happening.

When we're listening to the voice of fear, we're generally disconnected from the light within. This voice often brings on feelings of insecurity, nervousness, anxiety, or even sheer panic. Again, while it really doesn't feel right to listen to this, it's the loudest and most persistent voice when our minds are cluttered and noisy. It's as if we're in a fog, and we cannot see any light to find our way. As a result of all the fear, our minds are cluttered, and so we begin to *react* to life instead of *responding*.

It is only when you *quiet the mind* that you're able to hear the voice of love—that inner voice deep inside of you that connects you with the rest of the Universe. This voice does feel right and is always welcomed even if a disturbing message is brought forth. The voice of love is intuitive; it's an inner knowing. Still, many try to stuff away this voice because they're afraid of what it might be telling them. The voice of fear is often an unwelcome guest, yet it's really hard to ignore.

A few years ago while working with my own life coach, I was told a story that's attributed to the Cherokee. It's a story that will help you get in touch with your own feelings and understand which voice you are hearing. It goes something like this . . .

> One evening an old Cherokee told his grandson about a battle that goes on inside people. He said, "My son, the battle is between two wolves inside us all. One is evil: it comes from anger, envy, jealousy, sorrow, regret, greed, arrogance, self-pity, guilt, resentment, inferiority, lies, false pride, superiority, and ego. The other is good: it is joy, peace, love, hope, serenity, humility, kindness, benevolence, empathy, generosity, truth, compassion, and faith."
>
> The grandson thought about it for a minute and then asked his grandfather, "Which wolf wins?"
>
> The old Cherokee replied, "The one you feed."

After telling me the story, my life coach asked me which wolf I was feeding and which one I was starving. It was clear to see that I was feeding the wolf of fear, but the thought of starving anything didn't sit well with me. It seemed so cold and malicious, and I felt that the wolf of fear was serving me in some way. You see, I view the voice of fear as that child deep within me who's trying to look out for me so that I won't get hurt.

So I took a deep breath and decided that instead of starving either wolf, I would instead feed them both. What this means is that I choose not to beat up on myself and make the voice of fear evil. Instead, I lovingly recognize the voice of fear as a scared child. I listen, I feel my feelings, and then I quiet my mind so that I'm able to *respond* to the voice instead of reacting to it. It is then and only then that I am able to thank this voice of fear and tell the child within that we are safe and all is well. This allows the voice of love and my inner light to rise to sheer brilliance. You don't have to starve the voice of fear; you just need to learn how to respond to it. And you can only do that when you truly love yourself, feel your feelings, and quiet your mind so that your higher self can speak to you.

I know that life can get busy and it's easy to allow the mind to fill, but today, and every day, when you catch your mind filling with all of those random thoughts that are usually fear driven, take a breath, feel your feelings, and then quiet your mind to focus only on the present moment. If that's too hard, then stand back and watch an infant, a toddler, or an animal for just a few moments because very young children and animals spend most of their time in a mindful state. As we guide our children to shine their lights, let us remember that although we are here to guide them, they have much to share with us as well. One of the greatest gifts we can give our children is the gift of teaching them how to quiet their minds so that they can better hear the voice of love and "tune in" to their best selves.

CHAPTER 7

ESSENTIAL #4:

Tune In

"The present moment is filled with joy and happiness. If you are attentive, you will see it."

— THICH NHAT HANH

We live in a society that is consumed with technology and widely accepts disconnected behaviors. No matter where you are or what you are doing, stop and take a look at the people around you. I can almost guarantee that you will find someone texting, staring at a computer, or touching the screen of an iPad, iPhone, or some other electronic device. Either that or they're listening to music or watching TV. Most of these people are likely tuned out to what's happening next to them and tuned in to what's on the screen in front of them. We all know what this feels like.

The behavior in and of itself is not a horrible thing. And there's no denying that we all really do need to know at least a little about technology to be functional in the modern world. The problem arises when we become consumed by technology and our attention is taken away from the truly important things like the children who are watching, listening, and learning from our every action and reaction. Adults are constantly complaining that children are not paying close enough attention to their parents and teachers, but the real question is: are we adults paying enough attention to them?

Tuning in to the Children

Have you ever been driving in the car while listening to your favorite radio station when suddenly you start to lose the signal? The station begins to break up and, while you can sort of make out what the song is, there's so much static that you can't really enjoy it. This can be seen as an analogy of our lives as parents and teachers. Children are sending loud and clear messages—but due to interference of some sort or another, we're not always receiving them. And sometimes it's the adults sending the messages loud and clear, but they aren't always the messages we want our kids to hear. In both cases, this happens because we're not completely tuned in. I see this in schools and in homes every single day. It's difficult to focus on others or the world around us when we're not mindful. This is why it's critical to quiet the mind so that we can *tune in* to our higher self and the children in front of us.

Several years ago while conducting a parenting workshop—long before the iGeneration was born—I had a memorable example of this unfold right in front of me. We had just begun talking about tuning in to the people around us, when Sandy interrupted and began to talk about how frustrated she was with her 11-year-old son's lack of responsibility. She felt that he was not tuning in to her desperate pleas to just follow a simple direction. Every day her son would come home from school, drop his backpack on the counter, and continue on his way. This drove her crazy, and she'd told him countless times that she didn't want the backpack there. For some reason he continued with this routine despite his mother's requests. His behavior frustrated Sandy because she felt that she needed the counter space to prepare dinner, and she was annoyed that he wasn't paying attention to what she asked him to do.

It was obvious that this was a maddening situation for her, so I gave her the opportunity to vent a bit before I began to ask her questions about her day in general. I encouraged Sandy to walk me through a typical day in her life. Through her response, the real issue became blatantly obvious to everyone in the group—except Sandy. It took her a little longer to *see the light.*

Sandy was in a high stress job where she often felt compelled to take her work home with her in the evening. She woke early in the morning, made lunches for her children (often neglecting to make her own lunch), got the kids off to school, and then grabbed her own briefcase to head into the office. Her workday was typically hectic, with high demands placed upon her. Describing her homecoming at the end of the day, Sandy said, "I rush in the door every evening and immediately start preparing dinner. I don't even have time to really think about anything. It's like I'm a robot on autopilot!"

I nodded my head and said, "Yes, I can see how you would feel that way. Now, Sandy, you've talked about your briefcase and joked about how it weighs you down, right?"

"Oh, yes," she replied.

I continued, "Well, I'm wondering, just out of curiosity, if you could tell me where you put your briefcase when you rush in the door to get dinner on the table?"

She paused for a moment and then responded, "Well, I put it at the end of the counter so that I can get right to preparing dinner, and then after dinner I can complete the work that needs to be done for my job the next day."

I continued to nod my head and asked, "Is this the same counter that your son puts his book bag on?" I watched as everyone in the room smiled and nodded.

She looked a bit agitated and quickly responded, "Yes, of course! I don't have many counters to begin with, but my briefcase is out of *my* way!"

I saw that the smiles in the room turned to looks of sadness as the rest of the participants were beginning to see the whole story unfold. I again gave Sandy a few minutes to vent because now she was definitely feeling a bit defensive.

I then said, "Sandy, we are models for our kids 24/7, like it or not. If what you're telling me about your day is true, then it appears to me that you are like a hamster running on a wheel—busily going from one thing to the next, not actually noticing the people around you. Is it possible that your son is placing his bag on the counter—the same counter where you place your brief-case—in the hopes of getting your attention?"

She got ready to speak and then tears filled her eyes. Between sobs, she shared how she felt like she was losing her ability to be a good mom. Her husband worked long hours and traveled con-stantly. She had an eight-year-old daughter who also needed her attention, and she felt like her son was rebelling because his fa-ther wasn't around much. She explained how she'd recently been getting calls from school regarding her son's behavior and lack of attentiveness. She was feeling so overwhelmed that she couldn't really see what was actually going on.

I remember wrapping my arms around her in a hug and re-assuring her that she was still a good mom, and she just needed to find a way to get off the hamster wheel for a period of time each day in order to focus on tuning in to her children's needs and giving them the attention they were seeking. Sandy had never learned to quiet her mind. She didn't understand that if she calmed the noise in her own head daily, then she would be able to truly connect with her children and address her own needs as well. If she'd been taking time each day to be still and listen to the voice within, then she would have been able to tune in to her children's needs as well as her own. When we become mindful and learn to quiet our minds, it helps us all notice and connect with our family members and others around us. It's within the quiet that our senses are heightened and we're able to recognize the thoughts, needs, and feelings of the inner child and the loved ones around us.

If you think back to the story of Bella in Chapter 2, you may remember that her behavior could certainly have been labeled defiant. However, in reality, she'd actually been feeling quite lonely and just didn't know how to express that effectively. This is what often happens with our children. Because they're trying to block their feelings or stuff them away, they don't know what to do with the emotions when they actually come up. Instead of experiencing and processing them, kids turn feelings of hurt, anxiety, or disappointment into what appears to be defiance.

When we're mindful with our children, we're able to teach them how to be in the present moment and how to *respond* to life rather than reacting to it. We take the time to look beyond the present behavior and we *tune in* to what's truly going on with them. In order to do this, we too must be mindful instead of mindfull. Unfortunately, it's difficult to teach our children this lesson if we're sleepwalking through life.

Sleepwalking

One evening after leaving school, I was walking around the supermarket, picking up a few things I'd forgotten for dinner. As I looked around me, I couldn't help but notice how the other shoppers seemed to be moving in and out of aisles like drones. It seemed everyone was either looking down (avoiding eye contact) or staring straight ahead as though they were on some sort of mission. I was so curious about this behavior that I paused for a few moments to really take it all in. People were getting really angry about the little things, like long lines and price checks. Everyone seemed to be in a hurry. I smiled, knowing that some days I felt the exact same way; but I felt really lucky to be in a mindful space on that particular day. I wanted to remember what the other shoppers in the store looked like so I could recall this image when I felt myself going to that dark place.

I picked out the groceries I needed and made my way to one of the long lines. As I was patiently waiting my turn, I caught the eye of a toddler in the cart in front of me. She had life dancing in her eyes and was smiling as we looked at one another. I smiled back and thought, *Oh, you see the light in my eyes amongst all of these drones—how wildly exciting!* As that thought crossed my mind, she giggled out loud. It was really profound. I felt like we were the only two human *beings* in the store at that moment and everyone else had, unfortunately, become human *doings*. I began to feel sad as I looked around the store again and noticed all of the other little children with life dancing in their eyes accompanied by parents who were listless and staring ahead into emptiness.

What were we teaching these kids by modeling this behavior?

For years I'd wondered why children always smiled when they looked at me. I remember asking my nephew when he was about eight and he said, "Oh, that's easy, Nuni. You have sparkles in your eyes!" At the time, I thought that was cute. But as I looked around at the people in this market, I suddenly realized what those kids were seeing when they looked at me—it was the light within. Thank God for that bright light sitting in the cart in front of me. If it weren't for her, I might have morphed into one of those drones as I stood in line that evening.

Now it's time to be completely honest with yourself: how often do you find yourself sleepwalking through life? Do you a feel like a drone at times? When we're in those states, we're in that human *doing* mode, going through the motions rather than actually *living* our lives. In this condition it's nearly impossible to experience self-love or allow your feelings and emotions to flow. As a human *doing*, we typically feel incomplete and imperfect—always seeking to fill the void with things outside of ourselves. It would make sense, then, that if we're sleepwalking through life, we're *disconnected* and likely missing the cues that our children are sending. In essence, we are not tuned in.

Mindful Children

Children are typically curious and have natural receptors for what is going on around them. They have that innate ability we discussed in Part I to read the energy around them. As parents and teachers, we unfortunately have the power to shut this down by modeling disconnected behaviors. But do we really want to do this?

There are a number of reasons why we want our children to be tuned in to the world around them. For starters, we want them to listen to the voice within—what I call the light inside—so that they can make decisions based upon what *feels* right. We also want them to be sympathetic to others while protecting and loving themselves. And we want them to really live life rather than just existing.

This is the essence of a mindful child—a child who lives in the present moment, is in touch with his or her feelings, and consistently tunes in to the voice of love that resides deep within. This child is able to connect with the higher self by quieting the mind and then connecting with others around them instead of walking through life like a drone.

You know that no one starts off being completely disconnected. This is a behavior that's learned over time. We often disconnect from the world around us as we stop loving ourselves. When we begin to question our own value and worth, we start to believe we're not lovable. We stuff our feelings in order to get on with life and make others happy. We give our power over to fear and allow our minds to exist in a state of constant noise. In order to survive in this self-imposed state, we disconnect. This may seem easier than taking the time to create a mindful state—but where does it lead us?

When we're not mindfully tuned in to ourselves and others, we often have trouble allowing deep, meaningful relationships to take shape. We experience only superficial interactions and give our power away to fear. We run from one thing to the next, constantly trying to prove our worthiness. We get stuck in the addiction cycle or fall into a deep depression because life is just too hard. It's most difficult to create mindful children when we ourselves are not mindful. And if our children aren't mindful, then they will never be able to tune in to the light within themselves or others.

Tuning In

We all know what it feels like to have a growing to-do list and seemingly no time to get everything done. Believe me, I feel like I'm running on that hamster wheel more often than I care to admit. But no matter how crazy life may seem, it's essential that we take the time to really look into our children's eyes and listen to them in the moment. We simply have to find the time to really *be* in the moment with them as often as possible. When children come to us with complaints or hurt feelings, we're often quick to brush them off and continue what we're doing. But it is in these moments that we're actually creating *their* core beliefs and giving them tools to use for the future.

You see, we can't really complain when our children ignore us if we are, in fact, ignoring them. They won't learn how to give someone "full body attention" (where the whole body is focused on the other person) until we demonstrate it for them again and again. When your child comes running through the door and wants to read a story to you or desires to show you a picture they made in school, don't just half listen to the first sentence or glance at the picture and offer some generic praise. Instead, take a moment to stop whatever you're doing, square your body toward theirs, get to their eye level, and tune in by being mindful. Take the time to really hear what they're sharing with you and then offer a positive comment or question that will encourage them to tell you more. Try: "Wow, I really love this picture! Can you tell me about this shape at the bottom?" Or you could say, "That's a great story—I like how you used our family in it." Talk to them in detail, so they know that you're really listening.

If you take the time while your children are young to listen to them as attentively as possible, I guarantee you that this will impact their ability to love and value themselves as they grow up. We learn how important we are from our parents, teachers, and early childhood caregivers. I realize that there may be times when you cannot stop what you're doing completely to tune in to your child. This is okay! In those moments, simply tell your child that you will give them your undivided attention as soon as you're done with whatever it is that you're doing. Just please make sure that you do actually give them the attention you've promised when the time is right. If you leave them hanging, they'll interpret this to mean they're not important to you or not worthy of your time.

If, on the other hand, your child is exhibiting defiant behavior or negative attention seeking, it's important to stop for a moment before reacting to that behavior. Take a deep breath and quiet your own mind so that you can tune in to their true needs (that are often hidden beneath the surface). Before you judge their behavior, center yourself and try to put yourself in their shoes. Take a deep breath and just feel their energy for a moment. Listen to the voice deep within you. Trust yourself to know what is going on with the child. Whenever my son or a child in my classroom is acting out, pouting, sulking, or just behaving in a way that's out of sorts, I try even harder to be mindful and tune in. It's just like tuning in to a radio station that's fading out—sometimes you have to get yourself back in range in order to hear what's being said. I can guarantee that if you make the effort, it will be a win-win for both of you.

Children learn from our model, so if we're going to complain that they aren't good listeners or good at paying attention, then we also need to be willing to look at where they picked up these behaviors. We need to be open to tuning in to their needs and listening not only with our ears but also with our eyes and our hearts. The truth is, what our children may not be able to communicate through words, they often display through their body language and behaviors. We can only notice this if we're mindful and therefore tuned in to their thoughts, feelings, and needs that dwell *beneath* the surface.

Love yourself by feeling your feelings, quieting the mind, and then tuning in to your inner light. Love your children (or the children you serve) by tuning in to their frequency. Tune in to their needs, wants, and desires. Tune in to their pain, sadness, and discomfort. Then trust your higher self to know what's right in guiding them to honor the light within by listening to the voice of love deep within yourself. Mindfulness is a practice. It begins by taking a breath and being aware of that breath. The more you practice, the more you'll find yourself able to tune in and the more readily you'll catch yourself when you're tuning out.

Yes, it's true that we live in a disconnected society, but that doesn't mean it's impossible to reconnect. Giving our children a strong foundation means teaching them that we're connected to them. It means demonstrating to them that they are seen and heard. When we tune in to our children, we are giving them a gift. And the resulting joy and happiness they feel will impact the rest of their lives.

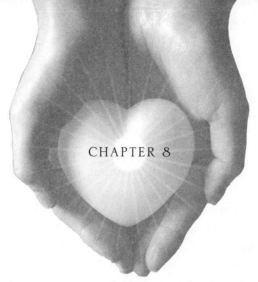

CHAPTER 8

ESSENTIAL #5:

Remove Toxic Thoughts

*"Most of us are just about as happy
as we make up our minds to be."*

— ATTRIBUTED TO ABRAHAM LINCOLN

Have you ever paid attention to your thoughts? Have you stopped yourself in the middle of the day to review your own thoughts and reveal how much of your thinking is negative and how much is positive? I often ask my clients to do this—to survey their thoughts. I simply ask them to become more mindful of what they think throughout the day and determine if most of their thoughts are driven by love or fear. Unfortunately, the majority discover that fear is in control, creating tons of toxic waste in their minds and hearts.

Several reports on metacognition reveal that the average person has anywhere from 30,000 to 70,000 thoughts per day, and approximately 80 percent of these are negative. As discussed earlier, a belief is simply a thought you keep thinking. Well, if your beliefs come from your thoughts and your thoughts are mostly driven by fear, then you could assume that many of your beliefs are going to be toxic in nature. Toxic thinking leads to toxic beliefs, which ultimately lead to toxic experiences. Is that what you truly want? Better yet, is that what you want for the children in your life?

Toxic thinking starts at a very young age. I listen closely to the words of the children I interact with, and I do my best to encourage them to replace negative words like *should, can't,* and *won't* with more empowering words like *could, can,* and *will.* My students learn very early on that every sentence we speak is an affirmation—a thought that we affirm to be true. The moment a student states a negative affirmation in my presence, I make it a point to teach them how to turn that thought around so they don't block themselves from their true potential.

For example, if I hear a student say, "I'm not good at math," I work with them to turn this thought into something more positive like, "I'm getting better at math every day." If they think that they aren't good at math, then every time we have a math lesson they'll feel nervous or uneasy. These feelings will support the thought that math is a struggle for them, and this will make it difficult for them to perform well during the lesson or on subsequent assignments. By shifting the thought, we begin to change the way we look at the situation and over time the negative belief that once held us back becomes long forgotten.

Negative self-talk doesn't serve us well in any situation, and therefore has no place in a child's daily curriculum at home or at school. The moment a child says something that can be perceived as a negative affirmation, I inquire, "Is that a good affirmation?" I follow up by asking them how it *feels* if they believe that thought to be true. If it doesn't feel good, then we work to turn it around. There's a terrific children's book by Byron Katie and Hans Wilhelm entitled *Tiger-Tiger, Is It True? Four Questions to Make You Smile Again* that I've used time and again to help teach children how to turn their negative thoughts around. I highly recommend this book for your personal classroom or home library.

My students learn to be mindful of their thoughts at the very beginning of the school year, and within a few weeks they're helping one another with this "turn around" process. It always makes me smile when I see them not only taking in the lesson for themselves but, more important, helping one another on this journey. I always find it amazing that six-year-olds can absorb this process so quickly—often more quickly than their adult counterparts. Perhaps that's because they have less toxic waste to release. They've had less time to internalize these negatives thoughts. The earlier we can teach children how powerful their thoughts are, the happier they will be in the years to come.

The Power of Thoughts

A few years ago my son suddenly became a fish in water and wanted to do more and more in the swimming pool. He saw the big kids jumping off the diving board and wanted to do that as well. But he was petrified because it was in the deep end, and he still didn't feel completely confident in his swimming skills. He spent weeks jumping into my arms in the shallow end to gain more confidence. After several jumps, he would casually say, "I'm going to the diving board now."

The entire family would stop what they were doing as he inched his way onto the board while I waited in the pool. His cousins, grandparents, aunts, and uncles would all encourage him, saying, "Come on, Nico, you can do it!"

But day after day he would come down off the board with tears in his eyes. "I can't do it, Mom. I just can't do it," he'd always say.

After several attempts, I pulled him to the side for a heart to heart. I remember looking into his big brown eyes as I held his tiny little hands and talked to him about the power of our thoughts. He'd heard this from me for so many other milestones in his life, like riding his bike for the first time, swimming without a flotation device, and drawing a picture of something he doubted he could draw. But in this moment, he needed to hear it once more. I gazed into his eyes and said, "Nico, honey, if you continue to get up on that board and allow your fear to overwhelm you, then you will *never* jump in. Instead of thinking *I can't do it,* let's turn it around by saying, *I can do this. I am safe. All is well and this is going to be fun!*"

He looked up at me, wiped his tears, and with a very serious look said softly, "But what if I drown, Mom?"

"Well, that's not going to happen because I am waiting to catch you in the water, and I am a super duper swimmer who's not going to let anything happen to my baby boy," I reassured him.

He paused for a moment, processing what I'd said, and then asked, "Well, what if my goggles fall off and I get water in my eyes?"

I responded, "Well, the good thing about eyeballs is that they're already wet, so if water gets in them we can simply blink and wipe it away."

He seemed satisfied, and then he blurted out, "What if my pants fall down?"

I laughed at this one and said, "I think that might be pretty funny, but if I tie them tight we shouldn't have a problem. However, if they still do fall down, is it okay if I laugh?"

He smiled and said, "You're crazy, Mommy."

I replied, "I know, buddy, and I'm all yours! Now, what are we going to say when we walk up to that board?"

I wanted him to come up with his own affirmation so he'd feel truly empowered. He looked at me pensively, put his finger to his chin and said, "I can do this. I believe in myself, and I know I can do this. Mommy is right here, my pants are tied tight, and I'm not gonna wear the goggles."

I looked at him and said, "Good choice, buddy. Let's do this."

He took his time to walk over to the board and creep toward the end of it. He turned away a few times as the fear resurfaced, and I encouraged him to remember his affirmation.

Then he looked at me and said, "Okay, Mom, I'm ready." He inched to the edge of the board and whispered, "I believe in myself. I believe in myself. I can do this."

Then he jumped straight into the deep end! As he popped up in front of me and I guided him toward the edge of the pool, I was the one who had to hold back the tears. He grabbed onto the side of the pool and was beaming with pride.

"I did it, Mommy, I did it!"

Yes, you did, my little man. Yes, you did.

We got out of the pool together and he asked to go to the board again. He looked at me and said, "Thanks for helping me to believe in myself."

Honestly, it was truly my pleasure.

The thoughts we think and the words we speak have a tremendous impact on our lives. For adults, the toxic thoughts come from core beliefs that formed long ago. However, for our children, there's a great opportunity to diminish negative core beliefs by teaching them early on how to turn their negative thoughts around. In doing so, we'll be creating a strong foundation that will help them navigate the waters of life as they grow. Our thoughts are more powerful than we often give them credit for, and once we realize this, we can make a huge difference in our own lives and the lives of our children.

Can't or Won't

When my son was standing in front of me with tears in his eyes feeling disappointed in himself and saying "I can't," it was my job to show him that it wasn't that he didn't have the ability to complete his task, but rather he wasn't *willing* to take the risk. There's a huge difference between *can't* and *won't*. If I say that I can't do something, I'm taking on the role of the victim, giving away my power. The feelings that arise with the words *I can't* are typically fear and helplessness. These words often trigger an emotional downward spiral.

My mom has been battling cancer for a number of years. I remember a time, several years ago, when she was told that the cancer had returned yet again. She was distraught and tired from fighting this disease for so long. As my mom, my dad, and I stood in the hospital after they told us that the cancer was back, her eyes welled up with tears and she said, "I can't do this anymore. I just can't."

I turned to her and said, "Okay, Mom, I understand."

She went on for a few moments and then looked at me and whimpered, "I can't do this. I just can't do this again."

I held her hand tightly and bravely said, "Mom, I love you and I know how hard this has been for you over the years. I have watched you struggle, and I have marveled at your strength. To me, you are amazing and you have a warrior spirit. If you are saying that you can't do this again, I will understand and accept that. However, I want you to know that it's not that you *can't* do this—it's that you *won't*."

She turned to me and said, "No, you don't understand. I *can't* do this."

I smiled and said, "It's *your* choice. You *can* do this. You can fight this once more, and likely win, because you are strong and you are bold. You have the ability to do this, but if you're too tired then it's okay. We will miss you, but I do understand that it's your body, your life, and your fight and there's nothing I can do to win this war for you."

She looked at me, this time with a puzzled expression, and said, "Gee, thanks. It doesn't matter if I die?"

"No, that's not at all what I'm saying," I told her. "What I'm saying is that the word *can't* is not the word to use here. You *do* have the ability to fight this and win. It's okay if you don't want to go another round. I totally understand, but the word to use is *won't*."

I believe that at this point she called me some sort of nasty name, but she was smiling when she said, "Huh. I guess I never looked at it that way."

Of course my mom wasn't about to say, *I won't do this again*, because she is too strong and determined to give up on life. She fought that battle, and a few more after that, and she kept on winning!

The Mind Is a Terrible Thing to Waste

While we spend a great deal of time figuring out how to best educate our children, we don't spend nearly enough time developing best practices for thinking. We try to teach our children *what* to think, but we rarely give them the tools they need to learn *how* to think. Toxic, negative thinking often turns the power of our minds against us. These thoughts hold us back in life and rob us of our true potential. Toxic thoughts surface when fear is in control, and they're like a tornado. They spiral out of control very quickly and are often destructive to our sense of self-worth, relationships with others, and overall happiness. If we want to give our children a strong foundation—and perhaps repair our own—we need to first become aware of our thinking. As I always say, awareness is the first step toward change.

To begin the practice of shifting your awareness, set aside a day, or even just a few hours in a day, to become mindful of your thoughts. Keep it simple. Use a journal or a blank piece of paper and make a "T-chart" at the top of the page. You can do this by simply drawing a large T on a piece of paper so that you're splitting the page in two columns, with a section at the top for titles on each side. Label one side of the chart "Negative Thoughts" and the other side "Positive Thoughts." Keep the chart with you, and throughout the day make a mark on it every time you have either a negative or positive thought. You may miss some, but you'll get a definite picture of whether you're being driven by love or fear. Be sure to note the various types of thoughts you have. Some may be simple thoughts that last just a moment. Perhaps you're looking in the mirror while you get dressed and you catch yourself thinking, *My hips are getting larger by the day.* Some may be fleeting thoughts that come and go multiple times throughout the day, such as *I'll never be good enough.* Take the time to really look at how your thoughts are shaping your experiences as you go about your routines. Then you'll be ready to look at alternatives.

Do you get frustrated when you have to stop in traffic and think, *Why do I always get the red lights?* Or do you feel thankful for the red light, seeing it as a moment to take in the sights around you or to pause and breathe. Toxic thoughts generally begin with a small thought like the ones above, and then grow and grow until we're stuck focusing only on what we don't want. They can be likened to weeds growing in the mind—if unattended, they'll spread like wildfire.

The Universe's Kitchen

Have you ever walked through a lunch line and been asked to quickly make choices as to what you want to eat? I recall the school cafeteria in both middle school and high school—and perhaps even elementary school if I strain my brain to remember. The lunch ladies had to get everyone served in a timely manner, so they'd stand there with their spoons filled and ready to serve, asking each passerby, "Do you want some?" You had to be quick with your answer, or whatever food was in that spoon ended up on your tray. There was no time to think about the decision. If you pondered for just a moment too long, the food was yours to eat.

Life is just like this. We're like magnets, drawing toward us what we affirm to be true. We're setting intentions without attention. If a good chunk of our thinking is negative, then we'll inevitably invite negative experiences into our lives, because just like the lunch ladies, the Universe has the spoon filled and is waiting to drop the contents on your plate. Therefore, be mindful of your thoughts because the Universe doesn't judge what you want; it just serves it up as you put in your request.

I once had a client who came to me because she was feeling a great deal of anxiety and believed she wasn't getting what she truly wanted in life. The first thing she was unhappy about was work. She hated her job and felt that it was keeping her from her two-year-old son. All she wanted was to be home with her child, raising him in her own way. She also wanted another baby, but was concerned because she had a difficult time getting pregnant the first time. She'd convinced herself that she would need medical intervention once again—something she obviously wasn't looking forward to. It was clear that I had my work cut out for me. Because her thoughts were so negative, she was creating hurdles and road-blocks for herself. At the same time, she was asking the Universe to help her uncover what her heart truly desired. This is when I taught her about the "Universe's kitchen."

I believe that we live in a Universe where God is a loving and nonjudgmental energy that never says *no* to us. Therefore, if you spend all of your energy focusing on how difficult it will be to conceive a child, the servers in the Universe's kitchen are sure to respond, *One difficult road to conception, coming right up!* It's just like the cafeteria ladies—they don't really care what you eat for lunch. If they hear you say, "Yes," they slap that food down on your plate without further thought. This is why it's critical to be aware of your thoughts. Because what you think about over and over again, becomes your reality.

Now, I don't want you to worry that every single thought that you think will instantly become your reality, because that is not how this concept (often referred to as the Law of Attraction) works. It's a misconception that fleeting thoughts create our reality. Rather, it's the repetitive thoughts—the ones that return time and again, every day. We need to be mindful of our most prominent thoughts because, as you now know, a belief is a thought that we keep thinking. The critical component of the Law of Attraction is belief. And when we think the same or similar thoughts over and over again, they do eventually become beliefs. When we become more mindful of our thoughts, we're able to shift the focus to what we truly *want* in life, rather than what we *don't want*. It's this tiny shift in perspective that makes all of the difference in our happiness.

The client I described continued to work with me for several sessions, and I helped her to change her thinking and release those toxic thoughts. It took a great deal of work on her part because she was inclined to hold onto the toxic core beliefs, despite the fact that they were ultimately holding her back in life. But all of her hard work paid off. (Please note: it doesn't have to be hard work. It's only difficult when we choose to hold onto the negative beliefs rather than releasing them gently. More on this in Part III.) We started with little things, like finding the perfect parking space when she pulled into the Target parking lot with her son.

After a few successes achieved as a result of shifting her thinking, she was ready for something bigger. As she worked to shift her thoughts toward what she *did want* from a work experience, she was able to let go of the job she hated and find herself a great opportunity that aligned more with what she wanted from life. Then we began to work on releasing the negative thoughts that were making conception difficult for her. Within nine months she had conceived her second child. I was very proud of her because in her mind it was hard work to change her thoughts, but she stuck with it and did the work. She realized that by shifting her thoughts she could actually change her life.

Choosing Positive Thoughts

What if we do, in fact, magnetize our thoughts into reality? What if there really is a Universal cafeteria line that we're all in— making choices unconsciously? Wouldn't it be more beneficial to make these choices mindfully and to teach our children how to do so as well?

If a child *thinks* they're not good in math or reading, they will have trouble performing in these subjects. The mere thought of working on an assignment will cause them to tense up, and they'll prevent themselves from achieving success. If a child *thinks* that they're not good at making friends, then they will refrain from reaching out to others and they'll inevitably feel left out. The cycle will continue until it becomes a belief. This is true with adults as well. If we *think* that we're not smart enough, then we'll constantly question our abilities and therefore validate this thought. If we *think* that there are no solutions to the primary issues in our lives, then we won't seek out a solution—or worse, we'll block the Universe from delivering the solution to us.

Our thoughts are powerful. If the majority of our thoughts are negative, then we're certainly drawing a lot of negativity toward us. Perhaps it's time to shift our perspectives and change 80:20 (80 percent negative and 20 percent positive) to 20:80. I'm not saying we have to constantly walk around with rose-colored glasses on and teach our children to do so as well. Rather, I am encouraging you to be mindful of your thoughts and words and understand that when we set intentions, we're better served by paying attention to what we want instead of what we don't want. This is a beautiful way to teach our children how to manifest their hearts' desires, and it certainly won't hurt us either!

CHAPTER 9

ESSENTIAL #6:

Speak Your Truth

"Stand before the people you fear and
speak your mind—even if your voice shakes."

— MAGGIE KUHN

Do you speak your truth? Do you dig deep to understand what is bothering you and why you are bothered by it, and then speak up for yourself to get your needs met? Many of us go through life simply reacting to situations rather than feeling our feelings, quieting our minds long enough to make sense of what's happening, and then responding. Even if we do feel our feelings and quiet our minds, often we have trouble speaking our truth for fear of what others will think, say, or do in response. This fear-based model of operating adds to those toxic core beliefs that we try so hard to eliminate. Speaking our truth is a critical component to leading a happy and healthy life. It's an amazing tool that we can teach to our children at a young age.

As a child, I heard the old admonishment "Children should be seen and not heard" far too many times. I can still remember how irritated I felt every time I heard someone say it. Those words made me feel invisible and unimportant, something no one likes to feel. Perhaps this is why I'm so driven to ensure the voice of our children is heard loud and clear.

Yet what actually is the voice of our children? In education we say that we're doing what's best for the kids. But who is to determine what *best* really means? Has anyone asked the kids what inspires them in learning or how they feel about all of the testing and data collection that's running rampant in our schools today? While the "children should be seen and not heard" saying may not be as commonly used today as it was when I was a child, the actions of parents and educators today indicate that, in many ways, we are still of that mind-set.

Think about it for a moment: when a problem or an issue ensues and a child tries to give input, do you listen carefully and sincerely or do you quickly dismiss it and ask them to be quiet while you work out the situation? I can think of several times when I felt pressure of some sort (usually due to a technical error with a computer or electronics) and my son tried to help. But because I was so caught up in the frustration I was feeling, I didn't trust him to find a solution. Nine out of ten times his input would have actually helped solve the issue—but I didn't listen.

I've learned from my mistakes over the years, and now I always make an effort to listen to the children when they speak. These little people are so pure of heart and mind that they're not usually as attached to the outcome as we adults are. They're able to share any idea that pops into their heads, rather than filtering to make sure it sounds cool or smart. Being less hindered by ego means their answers are inspired and quite often correct.

Listen to Children

When we get busy or we're operating out of fear, we have a tendency to *shush* the children in our lives. It's as though we have blinders on and can't stop, for even a moment, to look and listen to what is happening in the present moment. A long time ago, I learned—the hard way—how important it is to stop and listen to the children during times like these.

It was my first year teaching first grade in a new building. I'd taught almost every other grade, including kindergarten, but I was most accustomed to teaching children a little bit older in grades two and three. I'd been moved to first grade due to budget cuts. It had been several years since I'd worked with such young children, and I'd forgotten just how short their attention spans are and how much direction they actually need. The first few months were rough for me because I needed to re-acclimate to this age group. Usually, in the beginning of a new school year there are several fire drills. It was late October and I thought we were done with our quota for the first few months, but the fire alarm went off and caught us all off guard. We'd practiced the escape procedure what seemed like a million times but still, on this day, my students could not settle down and were extremely noisy throughout the process. During a school fire drill, it's important to exit the building in a quiet and orderly fashion. The kids usually do a great job because you work with them on this from the first day of kindergarten. But despite all the practice they'd had, my students were totally rambunctious on this particular day—perhaps it was a full moon!

The alarm went off right after recess, when of course the kids were still wound up from running amok outside. I summoned them to form a single-file line and go out through the door, but they simply would not stop talking. Some were even skipping out of the building, and I quickly noticed that I was getting *the evil stare* from the veteran teachers. This made me even more nervous. No one likes to be judged—especially when they're new to the school and the grade. I felt my blood begin to boil and my heart rate quicken. I was nervous and a bit annoyed. I don't like to *shush* my kids because it just seems so harsh and a bit rude to me, but on this day I felt I had no choice.

I remember one little boy kept calling out to me as we were walking across the pavement and onto the grass. I motioned with my hands for him to be quiet but he kept calling my name. I couldn't believe his defiance, and I shot him one of those evil stares that I'd been getting from the other teachers. Finally, the kids were all in line, quiet, and accounted for. I looked over at Mickey (the boy who had been calling out to me) and noticed the look of defeat on his face. I felt terrible, knowing his expression was a result of my ignoring his outbursts. However, I also felt justified because I was just trying to do my job. We waited quietly for a few minutes until they called us back into the building.

As we entered our classroom, I called the kids over to our meeting place and prepared to read them the riot act for their behavior. I began, "Boys and girls, what on earth were you thinking? When we go out to a fire drill it is very important that we are quiet so that we can hear the . . ." I stopped midsentence because I couldn't take the awful smell that had begun filling the room. I turned and looked around and then back to the kids and asked, "What is that awful smell?"

The kids shrugged their shoulders, but little Mickey slowly and tentatively raised his hand with a smirk and said, "I tried to tell you."

"Tried to tell me what?"

He smiled and said, "I tried to tell you that you were going to step in dog poop, but you told me to be quiet!"

With that, the whole class burst out laughing, even me. I laughed so hard that I had tears in my eyes—not only from laughter but also from humility. A few minutes later, two of the girls took my shoe to wipe in the grass just outside our door while I apologized to Mickey and the rest of the class.

It had been obvious to me that Mickey had something to say as we walked out during the fire drill, but I'd been so intent on getting those kids to quiet down—so that I wouldn't be judged by the other teachers—that I'd ignored his pleas and paid for it in the long run. I guess stepping in poop served me right. On that day I learned a valuable lesson: listen to children because they almost always speak the truth, if we give them the chance to.

Children Should Be Seen *and* Heard

Children are pure of mind and heart—if you can embrace this idea, then it's easy to understand why it's so important to give them the opportunity to talk about their feelings and speak their truth. If children are taught how to communicate effectively and given the opportunity to use their voices, then they're more likely to feel important and appreciated. On the other hand, if we shut them down by expecting them to harness their feelings or silence their words, it's possible to do insurmountable damage.

Every time I teach this essential to a group of kids I hear the same line: "No one wants to hear what kids have to say!" This tears me apart inside yet inspires me, even more, to give kids the tools that they need to be heard. When children are forced to stuff their feelings and mute their voices, their spirit or inner light begins to slowly diminish. Some children whose light has been dimmed may display characteristics of anxiety. Others may appear to be defiant, when truly their heart is aching and they are silencing their inner voice. Either way, if we took the time to really see and listen to these children, we could ultimately help them to under-stand their feelings and express themselves in a responsive and healthy way.

A New Way to Communicate

Lizzy was a bright light that bounded into the classroom every day with a new and exciting story to share. As the year progressed and we moved into the holiday season, I began to see some chang-es in her. I started to notice that she was a bit withdrawn and over-emotional. I watched her interactions with others for a few

111

days and noticed that she seemed to be on edge and wasn't fitting in with the other kids as she once had.

Something I like to teach my students in January of each school year is how to use "I Statements" to talk about their feelings. This helps them take ownership of a situation, voicing how they feel, why they feel that way, and what they need in order to feel better (responding), rather than blaming others (reacting). While I usually wait until the new year to teach this skill—because the kids in first grade are so young and limited in their writing abilities when they begin the year—I could see that Lizzy had something going on and that she needed an outlet. She loved to draw and she loved to write, so I pulled out my I-Statement worksheets and sat down with her one-on-one. (You can get one of these worksheets at www.thelightinsideofme.com/services by clicking the Parent Resources tab.)

I told her that I'd noticed her bright light appeared a bit dim lately. She hung her head and said, "I'm sorry, Mrs. Savini."

I put my hand under her chin to tip her face gently upward, looked in her eyes, and said, "Lizzy, you have nothing to be sorry for. I'd like to help you to brighten that light within once again. Would that be okay?"

She blinked her eyes and said, "I guess so."

I showed her my worksheet, and we worked through her very first "I Statement." It was at this point that it became evident to me that there was a great deal of turmoil in her home life, and she was struggling to find her way and remain a kid through it all. I stapled a bunch of the worksheets together, placed them in her daily work folder, and discussed when to use them.

It wasn't long after that Lizzy began asking for more sheets. Soon other kids began to take notice and wanted I-Statement sheets of their own. This is how my *I Feel Journal* was born. It was created for Lizzy and has proven to be a valuable tool in my classroom and empowerment camps ever since.

Lizzy was the type of child who appeared to do things to get attention and who would often be called a Drama Queen. This label is kind of like the Boy Who Cried Wolf—the little boy called for help so many times to get attention that no one believed him when he really did need help. Well, my student Lizzy was always telling stories and acting in such a dramatic way that soon her teachers, her recess monitors, and even her parents began to ignore her. Once Lizzy learned how to communicate her feelings effectively, however, she no longer felt the need to be overly dramatic—she was comfortable speaking her truth. She was able to simply express how she was feeling and why she felt that way, and also inform others of what she needed in order to feel better. This worked well not only for Lizzy, but for all of the students in my classroom. Still, sometimes we had to do a little tweaking.

I always have an I-Statement folder in my classroom, and I encourage the kids to take one and fill it out or draw a picture when they're feeling overwhelmed with strong emotions. They could be feeling anything from sadness and anger to fear or even excitement. Sometimes the students write the statement just to get it out of their system and then keep the paper as their own. Other times, they wish to share it and are looking for a resolution. On these occasions, the kids place the statement on my desk, which alerts me to the fact that they want to share it in a community meeting and try to solve the problem as a class.

One day Lizzy came in to school and immediately placed a completed I Statement on my desk. I assured her that we'd have a community meeting later that morning and discuss her feelings and help her through them. That put a smile on her face. Although it wasn't immediate satisfaction, she knew she was important and her feelings had been put on the agenda. When I had the time, I called the kids over for a community meeting. By this point in the day I had a few other statements on my desk as well. Lizzy's went something like this:

I feel sad
When Jeremy rips the picture I made for him
Because we are friends and that's mean.
What I really need is for him to be a nicer friend.

The kids were intrigued by this and probed further, asking for more information to help her out. It became clear that Jeremy was a child who lived in her neighborhood and attended our school but was in a different grade. Unfortunately, he was always "mean" to Lizzy, but she didn't quite understand this. She thought he was a friend, but he certainly wasn't treating her like one. Apparently, she had painted him a picture in the hopes of softening his heart, and when she handed it to him he said, "Yuck, that's ugly!" Then he ripped it up and threw it on the ground.

Several of the kids were shaking their heads as we discussed the story, and they looked quite disgusted. Then insightful little Jimmy looked right at Lizzy and said, "Lizzy, I get that you are sad because Jeremy ripped up the picture you made for him, but you said what you need is for him to be a nicer friend. Liz, you don't need him to be a nicer friend; you need a *new* friend!" The kids all nodded in agreement.

Lizzy nodded her head too, knowing that Jimmy had just spoken the truth. She smiled and said, "You're right. He's not a good friend. No more pictures for him!"

I Statements Are for Everyone

It's quite easy to teach the first three components of an I Statement, but the challenge comes in the fourth segment—the part that begins "What I really need is . . ." You see, we don't always know what we really need, and the truth is that we may ask for something and it may never happen. That's when we need to think about taking back our power. If my I Statement can only result in a happy ending if another person says or does something a certain way, then I may need to rethink it. In relying on someone else's response or action, I'm giving the power of my happiness over to someone else. On the other hand, if my I Statement helps me figure out what I need to feel better and isn't dependent upon another person, then I've just empowered myself. If I'm placing my happiness in the hands of others, then I may never truly be happy.

We're not truly loving ourselves when we are giving away our power and relying on others to help us to feel better. A more caring way is to make choices that feel good in our hearts and allow us to be our absolute best. Lizzy learned that lesson with Jeremy. He probably wasn't going to make her feel better, so she had to shift her "need" to making different friends in her neighborhood who would be true friends and treat her well.

This was a great lesson for all of the kids because they saw that sometimes we ask for something that we think we need and then we find out that we need something completely different. The bottom line is that we need to be able to speak our truth by expressing how we feel, defining when we feel that way, determining why we feel that feeling, and then stating what we need to feel better to be our absolute best. If that need can't be met, then we shift gears so that we can feel better and be our very best with a different outcome. This is one of the ways we can achieve self-love. Instead of waiting for others to brighten the light within, we own our power and choose to brighten it ourselves.

I Statements are powerful because they help individuals to voice their opinions without blame. For years they've been used for adults in conflict resolution, and I believe that if we teach our children how to use them early on, they'll become better communicators as they get older. (I give specific exercises on how to use I Statements in Part III of this book.)

In the case of Lizzy, she stayed away from Jeremy for a while and then he slowly came around and wanted to know why she didn't want to play. She told him that it was because he was mean to her and she only played with people who were nice to her. They tried playing together a few more times but Jeremy just couldn't help but bully Lizzy. I'm proud to say that she made the choice to keep her distance from him even when he said that he was going to be nice. By the end of the year if you'd asked her about Jeremy, her reply would have been, "Jeremy who?"

Words Are Powerful

Children are pure of heart and mind. They don't usually have a hidden agenda, unless of course you're standing in Target and they're vying for a toy that they absolutely don't need. They usually say what they mean and mean what they say—if they're given the opportunity to do so.

When I asked my son what he thought was important to share in this chapter he said, "Tell them to speak their truth."

I replied, "I know buddy, but what does that mean?"

He stated the same thought several times and then said, "Well mom, you know . . . tell them that it's important to talk about what you're thinking and feeling so that you're not keeping it inside, because words are powerful." He then told me to make sure I told everyone to be sure they weren't afraid to speak their truth because "if you don't tell people what you're thinking or feeling, how will they actually know?"

Let's be honest, children generally speak the truth unless they've been taught to silence that truthful voice. It's critical that we take the time to not only see our children for who they are, but also to listen to them—the inner voice and the outer voice. Our children will have more trouble speaking up if they're fearful or don't know how to communicate effectively. Good communication skills are one of the most powerful tools we can give our kids. Imagine what life would be like for you if you had been given this tool at a young age. I know that my life would have looked different. For starters, I wouldn't have been the little girl who was always pushed around. It took me a very long time to find my power, even though it was always right there inside of me. But once I found it, I knew that my greatest gift was the ability to teach others how to connect with their own power—the light within.

The upside is that it's never too late to heal the child within, and you too can communicate with I Statements, even when *your* voice shakes. Again, I will guide you through this in Part III.

CHAPTER 10

ESSENTIAL #7:

Plug In

*"At the moment of commitment the
entire universe conspires to support you."*

— ATTRIBUTED TO JOHANN WOLFGANG VON GOETHE

In November 2009, I hopped on a plane from New York to Tampa to attend a Hay House I Can Do It! conference. Something deep inside of me told me I had to go—even though I couldn't find anyone to go with me and I really couldn't afford it. In some strange way it just felt like I was supposed to be there. I'm delighted that I chose to listen to the voice within, because it was an awakening experience for me in so many ways.

Upon my arrival in Tampa, I had a nauseating feeling in my stomach and just knew that something was wrong back home. My husband had addiction issues that he never truly healed, but I'd convinced myself that they'd somehow disappeared. Honestly, I knew deep within that if he only stopped the behaviors but didn't take the time to heal his heart, the addictions would appear again.

Nevertheless, I was hopeful that he would defeat the odds. Unfortunately, the feeling in the pit of my stomach was a clear sign that upon my absence, he had relapsed. This "knowing" put me into an emotional tizzy. I'd called home and knew that my son was safe because he was with my in-laws, but I had no idea where my husband was or if he was okay. He wasn't returning any of my calls or texts—typical engaged addict behavior.

That evening Dr. Wayne Dyer was the keynote speaker, and even though I was in total emotional distress, there was no way in hell that I was going to miss his talk. We all sat mesmerized by Dr. Dyer as he enlightened and enchanted us with his stories and wisdom. I felt completely connected to both him and his message; as he shared stories of his family, I was taken back to my own memories of camaraderie with my family. I felt warmth in my heart as I listened to him talk about his relationship with his daughters. He had a playful relationship with his girls like my sisters and I had with my dad. Then, about three-quarters of the way through his speech, he announced that he'd recently been diagnosed with leukemia. The crowd was silent, and I remember feeling a piercing pain in my heart as a thought rapidly came to me. I placed my hand on my chest and thought, *Oh my God. What if that was my dad?*

Later that evening I discovered that my husband had in fact had a relapse, but was now safe at home. I knew I'd have to deal with all of it when I got back, but I was grateful that my son was safe and the truth was revealed with my husband. I spent the rest of the weekend on an emotional roller coaster and was anxious to get home and deal with the issues at hand.

On Sunday—my last day at the conference—I was sitting in the back of the convention center listening to one of my favorite speakers, Sonia Choquette, but feeling like I was jumping out of my skin. As I felt the anxiety rise, I thought for sure it was because I was anxious to get home and face my fears. Then, I heard a tiny voice inside of me say, *There's a Hay House book in you.* I shook my head and tried to refocus my attention on Sonia. A few minutes later I heard the voice again even louder this time: *There's a Hay*

House book in you. My skin felt like it was crawling, and I began to wonder if anyone else was hearing this voice because it was so loud and blatantly obvious to me. I took some deep breaths and refocused once more. Not long after I heard the voice yet again—this time in a very firm and loud tone: *There's a Hay House book in you!*

At this point I stood up and went outside to stand by the water and get some fresh air. Water always seems to balance me because I'm a Pisces, and I was looking for relief from this strange energy. After taking some deep breaths and calming myself down, I realized that I wasn't feeling anxiety from the mess I was going back home to. Rather, it was excitement. I've chased a lot of dreams in my life, so I literally said out loud, "If this is true, you'll need to bring it to me. I'm not chasing this." I then heard the tiny voice inside say, *Just be willing.*

I flew home that evening and talked with my husband to make some sense of what had happened with him. After our talk, I remembered the voice at the conference and made a conscious effort to be willing. For three days I walked around my house repeating the mantra, "I am willing." On the third day, after putting my son to bed, I was compelled to go to my office and sit at the computer. I almost immediately began typing. I wasn't sure what I was writing, but I just let my fingers do the walking as the words poured through me. I worked for over an hour and when I looked at the clock I noticed that it was 10:30 in the evening. I suddenly realized that I was tired as a deep yawn came from me. I sat back in my chair with a feeling of satisfaction because the next day was Thanksgiving and I simply couldn't wait to go back home to spend the day with my parents and share that I was writing a book. I went to bed with a huge smile on my face because I was listening to the voice within and being guided to do the work I was put here to do. I felt honored and also excited.

An Awakened Experience

I woke up at four o'clock in the morning the next day from a terrible dream. In the dream, I was standing in a cemetery and it was drizzling. My sisters and I were all dressed in black, standing in a semicircle, looking down at a casket in the ground. In my mind I assumed it was my mom because of her battles with cancer through the years, but then I looked up and saw my mom standing across from me, also dressed in black. I then understood that it was my dad in the casket. I woke up in a fierce panic. I was sweating and panting like a dog. I took a few breaths to settle down and tried to tell myself it was only a dream. Then I noticed my son standing by my bed rubbing his eyes. At the time he was only four years old. I turned toward him and asked what he was doing up so early.

He looked deep into my eyes and said, "I had a weally bad dweam." I pulled him into bed to snuggle with me and talk about it. Whenever he has bad dreams we talk about them, put them in an imaginary bubble or a balloon, and then release them to the Universe. This time, however, when I asked him to tell me about the dream, he looked deep into my eyes once more and said, "I can't tell you this one, Mommy."

That was when I knew that it wasn't just a bad dream. Instead, it was a message from the Other Side. Perhaps it was our angels, spirit guides, or ancestors who were trying to forewarn us of what was to come.

We fell back to sleep together until the phone rang at 7 A.M. Sure enough, it was my mom telling me that my dad was in the hospital, and he'd been rushed there at the same time that I'd retired to bed with a smile on my face the night before. I spent the next few days by my dad's side, trying to stay positive and be hopeful. Because it was Thanksgiving weekend, it was hard to get test results to find out exactly what was going on. Finally, after several phone calls to the lab and desperate pleas for help, the doctors concluded that my dad had leukemia and another form of cancer called mantle cell lymphoma (MCL), which is apparently pretty rare and very lethal.

From the moment the doctor mentioned the word leukemia, my dad was fixated and zoned in on it. He kept saying, "My grandfather died of leukemia." I knew it wasn't good that he kept focusing on that, because his thoughts were turning to a belief that he too would die from this. I'd studied Reiki—a hands-on healing energy practice—for years, so I immediately began giving him Reiki treatments and played CDs by Louise Hay via headphones in an effort to lift his spirits and shift his thoughts. I soon noticed that it was too late because the negative thought had been planted, and he continued to spiral downward mentally, physically, and spiritually as he focused upon his demise.

I drove back and forth to the hospital for a few days, and then on Saturday evening my dad asked me to go home and be with my husband and son. I dreaded the thought of leaving his side, but I knew that he was right—I needed to go home to be with my boys. I drove home that evening and had a very difficult time staying awake. I listened to Wayne Dyer's *Excuses Begone!* audio CD to keep me alert and to keep my mind off thoughts of the inevitable. I spent time with my boys and then went up to the healing room in my home (which is the room I use to coach my clients) to do some long-distance Reiki on my dad.

I called my mom around 9 P.M. to check in on her. As we talked on the phone, she received another call. She abruptly came back to the line and said, "Vick, I've got to go. It's Daddy." My heart raced as I waited for communication from my mom or my sister who lived in our hometown. I wanted desperately to jump back in the car, but knew it wasn't safe since I'd had such a hard time staying awake on my drive home. An hour later my mom called to tell me that my dad had a heart attack. He was stable but unconscious. My sister told me to get some rest and plan on coming back in the morning. She promised that she would call me if there were any change.

It was difficult to fall asleep because I was full of fear, but I eventually passed out from exhaustion. I was then awakened at

2 A.M. by my sister's phone call. I was shaking as I answered the phone, and I heard my sister say, "Vick, you've got to come." My husband and I jumped out of bed, called my in-laws to come to the house to be with my son, and hurried to get ready as quickly as possible to drive back to my hometown—90 minutes away.

As I walked out of my bedroom, I heard my son talking in his room. He sometimes talks in his sleep but I thought it was odd, so I walked closer to see if I could hear what he was whispering.

My son hadn't been allowed into the hospital to visit my dad because there was a flu epidemic, and the hospital chose to keep all children out of the intensive care unit. I'm not sure what their reasoning was, but I couldn't see my dad without a protective mask as an adult, and the kids were simply not allowed in this area of the hospital. My dad was disappointed that he couldn't see his grandchildren to talk with them so I'd taken a video of my dad for Nico earlier in the day to give him a message from his grandfather. Suddenly, I remembered this video and thought about what my dad had said: "I'll see you soon, buddy. Don't worry. I love you!"

As I approached my son's room, I heard him clearly say, "No, Papa, I can't play right now. I'm just too tired."

I ran down the hall and told my husband that we needed to leave immediately because I felt that my dad was already transitioning. My in-laws arrived within minutes, and we were on the highway.

I spent the next five hours standing by my father's side, watching him lie in the white hospital bed unconscious. I prayed, used healing touch, whispered messages in his ear, and sang to him. My dad always loved it when I sang. I looked at the machines attached to him and watched his vital signs dropping. Still in disbelief, I kept hope in my heart that some miracle would happen and this would all just be a bad dream. My whole family sat around, feeling helpless, and the tension began to mount. We all began to panic around the same time, realizing this wasn't going to turn around. I remember the heat rising in the room and an argument ensuing over what to do about his care—send him to a larger medical facility or keep him where he was. My mom began to cry and started to talk to my unconscious dad.

She whimpered, "Savie, I don't know what to do. I don't want to do the wrong thing here and I can't make this decision alone."

I placed one hand on my mom's heart and the other on my dad's. I remembered how much my dad loved the movie *The Godfather.* For some reason that popped into my head, so with one hand on my mom's heart and one hand on my dad's I said, "Mom, Dad is not going to let you make this decision. Right now he's making God an offer that cannot be refused."

Of course then I realized that perhaps my dad was the one getting the offer. I leaned close to him and said, "Dad, I know that right now you're making deals with God and trying to make an offer that cannot be refused, but maybe you should ask what life would be like here and then what life would be like there. I don't want you to go, but I trust you to know what's right for you."

I kept one hand on his heart and placed the other above his head. I was still waiting for a miracle as I stared at his skin, which was getting colder by the minute. After a few minutes, I began singing "Over the Rainbow," and toward the end of the song, I noticed his breathing had changed. I stared right at him, taking in his magnificence as I held him in my arms, and then it happened. He took three deep breaths and transitioned from Earth.

Disconnected

That's it. He was gone. I was holding on to his lifeless body but he was no longer right there, in that bed breathing and alive. For days, I'd been so strong, but in that moment I regressed to a little girl. The pain in my heart was so immense that I fell to the floor in a puddle of my tears. The next few months formed the most difficult time period of my life. With all I knew in my heart and all I'd learned over the years about Spirit and the energy of the Universe, I still couldn't pull myself out of this deep, dark depression. Sure I put on a smile during the day like a piece of clothing, but at night

I cried for hours before falling asleep. I was thinking negatively most of the time. Sometimes it felt like 99 percent of my thoughts were negative. Every day I got up and did what I had to do. I existed. I went through the motions of life, feeling every sorrowful emotion a person could possibly feel. Weekends were the worst because I wasn't teaching and didn't have the distraction of 20 first graders needing my constant attention and support.

One Saturday afternoon I went into my healing room. As I walked through the door, all I could think about was that somehow I had to snap out of this funk. I was sick and tired of feeling sick and tired, and I knew that my dad probably wasn't very happy with me carrying on in this way. I was feeling so negative that any small event seemed catastrophic to me. I flipped the switch to turn on the floor lamp in the room, and there was a flicker—but then the lamp went out. My response was, "Great. The damn lightbulb burned out."

I ran downstairs to get a replacement and then changed the bulb. I flicked the switch and nothing happened. I thought, *If it isn't the lightbulb, then what the hell is it?*

There's a futon in that room, which is normally set up like a couch for clients. But on this day, for some reason, it was extended into its bed position. I plopped down on it, feeling annoyed and disgruntled and believing that life truly sucked. As I lay on the bed full of anger, sadness, and despair I somehow noticed that the plug in the wall was loose. It was halfway in the socket and halfway out. I paused for a moment because for some reason this seemed significant. I felt a sensation run through my body from my head to my toes, and then the tears welled up in my eyes. I finally got it—I had disconnected from Spirit. In all that I'd been through over the past few months, I had turned away from Source energy. The energy was always there and available to me, but I simply wasn't plugged in.

Source energy, God, Spirit—whatever name floats your boat— is always available to us just like electricity from wall outlets. Each person has a light inside their heart that connects them to all of humanity in mind, body, and spirit. We each have our own energy supply, but like all energy, it starts to drain if it's not replenished or recharged. So when you're feeling stress, fear, anger, resentment, or depression, you're working in high gear and burning up a lot of that energy. If you don't replenish it, you'll be heading for disaster—mentally, physically, and most important, spiritually.

A car can't run without gasoline. A mobile phone will go black if you don't plug it in to recharge the battery. We are quite the same. We need Source energy to sustain us and keep us moving forward toward the bliss that we so truly desire and absolutely deserve. To me, Source is God, Creator, Spirit, Creative Center, and Peacefulness. It is all and everything that surrounds and dwells within us. It's the only thing there truly is, and I've learned that it's all that actually exists. Source energy is always available to us. Your heart doesn't need permission or direction from you to pump blood through your veins throughout the day. Your lungs don't need your guidance to breathe the air that you need. Your body systems continue to do what they were intended to do (unless there's a medical disconnection) without your help or direction every single day of your life. The sun rises and sets. The air continues to flow. And the Earth continues to spin. We are always supported by the Universe. If you look around and realize how you're supported on a daily basis, it becomes clear that there's something much bigger than us out there somewhere—or perhaps deep within our very own hearts.

The question is: Do you connect with that energy? In other words, do you refuel your tank? For months after my dad transitioned, I wasn't filling my tank. I was running on empty, feeling angry, dark, and abandoned. Still, the Universe never stopped supporting me. It's just that I'd stopped noticing. Just like the plug hanging out of the wall, I wasn't properly plugged in to Source energy. My inner light was dim, and I was doing nothing to brighten it.

Connecting to the Light Within

When I decided to move forward with publishing my children's book, *The Light Inside of Me,* I knew that I didn't want an artist to illustrate it. Every time I closed my eyes and envisioned the completed version, I saw art created by children. It was clear to me that this book was for kids, and I wanted their interpretation of the words on each and every page. My solution was to have children from my school who wanted to submit a drawing choose the sentences they wanted to illustrate and then send in their creation. It was extremely difficult to choose which of all the beautiful and unique images I'd use in my book. The one thing that stood out for me was that each child illustrated "the light within" as something that radiated out from the heart. Children are so incredibly intuitive. While not one line in that book states that the light within comes from our hearts, they all somehow knew that it did. I remember sitting back in an old rocking chair that we'd used while holding my son when he was an infant and looking at all of the pictures. I was thrilled—the kids got the message without me having to directly say it.

As I described earlier, my children's book was written as a poem several years prior to its publication, to help a very angry little boy learn how to deal with his feelings and make choices based upon how they felt in his heart. As it says, "Deep inside me is a light that burns and glows and shines so bright. To make my light shine bright, I make good choices and do what's right . . . when my light is dim, I know it's time to look within." I believe that just those few simple lines of the book define the light within—it is your highest and best self.

The beautiful thing is that you can refuel, plug in, or connect to Source energy to brighten this light in many different ways. Some people connect through prayer; others connect by communing with nature. Some get in touch with their creative side by drawing, writing, painting, or creating music. To plug in, all you need to do is connect with that part of you where everything flows naturally. We connect with the light within when we're doing what *feels* right in our hearts, when we do what we were meant to do. We make this connection when we're being true to ourselves and honoring the voice within. Once we're plugged in to Source energy, we know that we're supported and can trust the flow of the Universe. Even when bad things happen, we have an understanding that this is all in Divine order; and so as difficult as it is to accept these situations, we get through because we know that it's going to be alright in the long run.

Most children aren't taught how to connect to this light within. We live in a disconnected era that's breeding violence in every corner of the world. We not only hear stories of bullying and violence in our schools, but we watch massacres unfold in front of our eyes in schools and public places across the globe. If we all taught our children how to plug in to this inner light and the importance of connecting to one another, then perhaps bullying, random violence, and rampant anxiety wouldn't be issues.

We need to teach our children and remind ourselves that when our inner light is dim, we can brighten it simply by connecting with Source energy and recharging. It doesn't matter how you connect: attend a church, temple, spiritual group, or inspiring lecture; read a book; paint a picture; walk in nature; or express yourself artistically. What matters most is that you know that we are always supported, Source energy is always available, and we are all connected by the beautiful light inside of us.

In the next section of this book you'll be given methods that I have used for years so that you can put these 7 Essentials into practice in your home, your classroom, and above all, in your own life. You've been given a deepened awareness of the importance of childhood and shown alternatives for creating a strong foundation for your children and yourself. Now get out your toolbox for life, and let's add some tools to ignite the light!

PART III

BE
THE
LIGHT

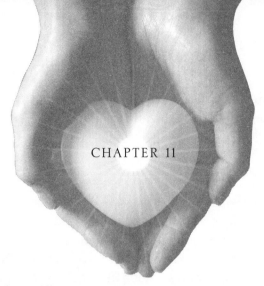

CHAPTER 11

A LOOK IN THE MIRROR

"True beauty is looking in the mirror
and smiling back at what you see."

— AUTHOR UNKNOWN

How often do you look in the mirror? Most people wake in the morning and are immediately in a rush to get off to work or otherwise begin their day. The majority of us pause momentarily to look at our skin, tend to our hair, brush our teeth, or look over the outfit we're wearing for the day. We merely glance at our reflection, but most of us don't truly look into the mirror. You see, I'm not interested in how frequently you eye the image in the glass hanging over the sink or above the dresser. Instead, I'm asking if you're being mindful of what's occurring in your life and if you're taking the time to "look" within to discover the inner light that reveals your very best self. If you're feeling stuck, frustrated, or stressed about any aspect of your life, chances are you're not really looking in the mirror. If you're ready to move forward in life, find peace within yourself, and be your absolute best, then I invite you to take a deeper look into the mirror of life.

A Deeper Look

You are an amazing manifestation of life, and you have something wonderful to contribute to this world. Yet I ask you, do you know this? Throughout your life—up to this very moment—you've been given reminders of who you truly are. But if you've never taken the time to really look into the mirror, you might not recognize, realize, and openly respond to your true self. When you're expressing your true self, you create the bliss that you so deeply desire and certainly deserve. And isn't that exactly what we all want?

Several years ago, I read *The Law of Attraction,* by Esther and Jerry Hicks, whose work I've mentioned throughout this book. It enticed me, enchanted me, and even entertained me—yet I didn't fully comprehend the concept at that time. *The Law of Attraction* is a remarkable book that was channeled to the authors by Spiritual beings. The poignant lessons teach us that our thoughts create the lives we live. Years later, *The Secret* came out, and it was all the rage. I smiled when I finished reading that book because it reminded me of *The Law of Attraction.* In fact, it was quite similar! *The Secret,* which was suddenly being talked about all over the mainstream media, served as a great reminder for me that my thoughts were ultimately creating my life. It also prompted a bit of an awakening for society, as many more people started to look deep within to find true happiness. Still, I wasn't able to fully grasp this Law of Attraction concept in its entirety. I just couldn't see how to make it work for me. I wasn't yet able to totally internalize the fact that I was one with Source (God), and I was co-creating every moment of my existence by aligning with this energy.

I didn't grow up believing that I could ever be one with God. I was brought up Catholic, with a great deal of religious fear and guilt (although that never quite resonated with me). Just before reading *The Law of Attraction,* I began reading books by Louise Hay—a true beacon of light in my opinion. My first encounter with Louise's work was reading her book *You Can Heal Your Life.* It touched my soul and made me really begin to think more consciously about my thoughts. Still, I didn't totally grasp the fact that I was actually creating my experiences. I didn't recognize how all of this mindful thinking and higher consciousness could possibly work for me and ultimately change my life.

I spent a great deal of time devouring any and all materials that would lead me closer to understanding my "true self," because I somehow didn't feel balanced—whole, perfect, and complete. I attended lectures, spiritual classes, retreats, and many different kinds of churches. I went to conventional therapists, hypnotherapists, psychics, energy workers, spiritual teachers, and Native American healers. You name it, I tried it! I did this because I so badly wanted to understand who I was and what my role was in this world. I wanted to know how all of the pieces of my life fit into the bigger picture and how I could become my very best self. The problem was that I was looking for answers *outside* of myself. Then one blessed and truly amazing day the *light* came on.

My True Reflection

I was always on a quest to find the perfect church. I'd tried so many different ones, always seeking my spiritual home, to no avail. On a bright and sunny Saturday morning, I stepped into a place called Unity Church. I walked down a long hallway as the sunlight was beaming through the windows. I felt the warmth of the sun and an unexplainable feeling of peace in my heart. As I continued on, I noticed many beautiful pictures hanging on the wall. I paused briefly at each one until I came to a golden picture frame with a white cloth cascading over it. Beneath this covered frame was a label that read, "The Christ."

Of course I was curious, but given my Catholic upbringing, I was also a bit frightened to lift the cloth because hiding a picture of Christ just seemed immoral. I stood there wondering what could possibly be under that cloth and why it was covered. All of my training in the Catholic Church came back to me, and I began to panic as I tried to understand why this church would hide a picture of Christ. I allowed my fearful thoughts to overwhelm me for only a few moments before I came to my senses and decided it was ridiculous to stand there and wonder what was under this cloth. Without further ado, I lifted the cloth—and to my surprise I found a mirror.

At first, I glanced at the surface of the mirror and was puzzled. I asked myself, *Why would a mirror be hanging here next to all of these beautiful pictures with a label underneath that says "The Christ"?* I looked at the mirror again—this time looking in it—and I saw myself. My physical features appeared to me as if I were looking in the mirror to get ready to go out in the morning. I paused for a moment, looked down the hall at the sunlight streaming into the windows then looked directly back into the mirror. This time I looked deep into my own eyes. It was then, upon the third look into this mirror labeled "The Christ," that I understood for the very first time in my life that I was in fact made of *God-stuff.*

As chills ran down my body and the tiny hairs on my arms stood tall, I felt overwhelming love. It suddenly appeared as though the sunlight streaming through the windows was a spotlight from Spirit, and this was my big day! It was then that I began to understand that we are all one with God and we certainly do co-create our lives with the Divine. For the first time in my life, I saw and consciously experienced the light within.

That day I found the perfect church for me, a place I could call my spiritual home. Except it wasn't a building that I could walk into, or even a religious sect. Instead, it was the beautiful gift of enlightenment. I finally understood that *I* was one with Spirit and *I* was co-creating with God. My spiritual home had been *within me* all along, and the mirror in front of me was no longer just a special pane of glass. Instead, it was an opportunity to be mindful and reveal my best self.

The MIRROR

The Spiritual awakening you just read about was profound for me in more ways than one. Believe it or not, for several years leading up to this experience, I was teaching a concept based on the acronym MIRROR—meaning **My Identity Recognized, Realized, and Openly Responded** to—that came to me as an idea one day. I began to use this as a means to teach individuals how to look at themselves with love instead of judgment and to learn how to go *with* the flow of life instead of against it. The MIRROR concept has proved to be a powerful way to help people connect to the light within.

Therefore, the very first tool I'd like to give you for your toolbox in life is this MIRROR concept. By making a commitment to yourself to practice the 7 Essentials described in Part II, you're ultimately looking deep into the mirror of life to reveal your best self. Several times in this book I've referenced how our thoughts create our experiences. The MIRROR concept is a quick and easy way for you to gain control over negative thoughts or situations and take your power back. Our thoughts create our experiences, and responding to life instead of reacting creates peace.

MIRROR is a simple "3R concept" with deep meaning that leads to a lifelong path of happiness and inner peace. The 3Rs aren't what you might expect from a teacher—reading, writing, and arithmetic. Instead, each stands for a different phase in our decision-making process: *Recognition*—becoming aware, *Realization*—acknowledging alternatives, and *Response*—taking action. When we take the time to quiet our minds we begin to look at life quite differently.

— **Recognition:** Step 1 of MIRROR is awareness. You might ask yourself, *Do I like what I'm feeling?* or *How did I get to this point?* In this phase of the MIRROR concept, you acknowledge the existence of your feelings. You quiet your mind, tune in to the voice within, and plug in to your higher Source. You take the time to recognize what's really going on in your life and how you may have created your current circumstances. You open your eyes and wipe them clean. You become mindful—present in the moment—and you allow yourself to view your truth. Whether you're in a good-feeling place or a bad-feeling place, you simply take off your blinders and acknowledge your state of affairs.

— **Realization:** Step 2 of MIRROR is acknowledging the alternatives to your current situation. You take a look at your circumstances as if you're a third party peeking in. You step back and review different options to bring yourself to a better feeling place. You ask yourself, *What can I do about this?* If you have difficulty seeing the alternatives because your mind isn't quiet, then you can seek professional guidance to gain insight into alternatives for your personal situation. But be careful not to simply go with what others instruct you to do. When you make decisions based solely upon what others tell you to do, they never feel right because you've given your power away. You still have to dig deep and go with what *feels* right to you. Otherwise, you're searching outside of yourself for answers.

— **Response:** Step 3 of MIRROR is taking positive action to move forward in your life. You are aware of your circumstances and you've looked at your alternatives, and now instead of reacting to life, you respond.

Most of my clients are able to recognize what's going on in their lives and where it all comes from without much difficulty. They can generally pinpoint their major core beliefs and tie them to specific events or overall messages taught in their childhood. Many are also able to consider alternatives to what they've done up until this point. They clearly realize that there are other choices available to them, but they're just not sure how to move forward and make critical changes for themselves. This is where I come in. I help them to respond differently than they have in the past, and I hope to do the same for you and the children you serve.

When you're truly mindful, you no longer *react* to life out of fear. Instead, you love yourself, feel your feelings, quiet your mind, tune in, remove toxic thoughts, speak your truth, and plug in to

Source energy—you take the time to *respond*. By making a commitment to yourself to practice the 7 Essentials, you're ultimately looking deep into the mirror of life to reveal your best self. You own your power instead of giving it away, and you hold yourself accountable to ignite the light within. The MIRROR concept is a quick and easy way for you to gain control over negative thoughts or situations. Our thoughts create our experiences, and *responding* to life instead of *reacting* creates peace.

Looking into the MIRROR

Let's take a deeper look at the MIRROR concept. As I said, the acronym stands for **My Identity Recognized, Realized, and Openly Responded to.** Your identity is who you believe you are. You may define yourself by the things that you do, what others tell you that you are, or how you feel about yourself. I believe that your current identity is simply an illusion, because you are so much more than you've ever given yourself credit for. Instead of beating up on yourself, questioning your connection to Source, or doubting the power that's deep within you, I encourage you to be mindful and respond to life. In this way, you'll not only ignite the light within, but more important, you'll be your absolute best. Your igniting the light in yourself will also ignite the light in the children who surround you—which is my ultimate goal.

Mirror Practice

This exercise will help you practice the MIRROR concept. In a journal, write the date and the following three questions:

1. Who am I?

2. What am I?

3. Where am I?

Take a few moments to answer each question, but don't overthink it. Give yourself about three to five minutes for each question and write what comes to your mind. There's no right or wrong way to do this because you're simply listening to your higher self and writing the first thought that comes into your mind. Now, turn the page, write the date and write these questions:

1.   Who do I *want* to be?

2.   What do I *want* to be?

3.   Where do I *want* to be?

Again, only allow three to five minutes for each question and write the first thoughts that come to mind. Here's an example of how the questions might be answered:

Page 1

1.   Who am I? *I am a woman who often feels like a scared little girl.*

2.   What am I? *I am teacher, a wife, and a mother.*

3.   Where am I? *I'm in the middle of a financial and emotional crisis.*

Page 2

1.   Who do I want to be? *I want to be a confident woman who speaks her truth.*

2.   What do I want to be? *I want to be my very best self.*

3.   Where do I want to be? *I want to be in this moment, feeling peace in my heart.*

On the next page—page 3—write the acronym for MIRROR at the top of the page like this: MI**RR**oR. Make sure that the R's are larger than the other letters. On the next line write the word

Recognize, and then next to that write, "I am aware. I am aware that . . ." Now, fill in the next few lines with what you are aware of. For example, *I am aware that I feel stressed most of my day because of my job and something has to give.* Write as much as you need to in order to understand your feelings and get to the heart of the issue that's bothering you.

Then skip four to five lines and write the word *Realize.* Next to that word, write, "I have alternatives. My alternatives are . . ." Take some time to quiet your mind before you do this step and then be honest with yourself. You might write something such as *I have alternatives. My alternatives are keep feeling this stress and end up sick, take a meditation class, seek a professional coach/counselor, begin to start the process in motion to find another job that suits me better.*

Finally—this is the most important step—skip four to five more lines and write the word *Respond.* Next to this word, write, "I create my life. I can take positive action. I will take action by . . ." For example, *I will take action by waking in the morning and taking a few minutes to just breathe. I will do this every day this week to center myself and quiet my mind. I will begin writing a list of what I want in my new job and start the process in motion to seek a new job by next week.*

Hold yourself accountable by placing this paper where you can see it every day. You can even rip out this third page and carry it with you. If you really want to be sure you'll follow through, then copy it and give it to a friend or partner to help you on your way.

This exercise is an example of the long process where you actually take the time to write out what's happening in your life. This is good to do when you first begin to use the MIRROR tool. However, you'll quickly get to a point where at any moment of the day you can stop yourself, recite the 3R's, and ask, *What's going on here? What alternatives do I have?* And, then take action!

By looking deeper into the MIRROR, you're practicing the 7 Essentials. You are loving yourself, feeling your feelings, quieting your mind, tuning in, removing toxic thoughts, speaking your truth, and above all connecting to the Divine light within. On the flip side of this, when you practice the 7 Essentials, you ultimately look into the MIRROR as well. The two concepts are lovers. They go hand and hand to guide you to your best self so that you can empower children to be their best selves!

Igniting the Light with MIRROR

I'm going to let you in on a little secret. This whole book is actually based on the MIRROR concept. Part I of this book was dedicated to bringing about a very important *awareness*. Chapters 1–3 were written to bring about the awareness that childhood is too precious to ignore. In that section, you were prompted to awaken to what's happening in our schools, homes, and society in general during this time period we call childhood. I hope that you also recognized the power of *your own* childhood and how it has affected your life thus far. The 7 Essentials were presented in detail in Part II and are *alternatives* that we can use to create strong foundations for our children while they're young, and to repair and strengthen our own foundation as adults. The final step of the MIRROR concept is to respond by taking action. You've already begun with the exercise in this chapter, and in the remaining chapters you'll have many more opportunities to take action by applying the simple tools I'll provide.

The reason I titled this book *Ignite the Light* is because I truly do believe that the children are our future, and if we want the best for them and from them, then we need to see the light within first. I believe that if we want to prepare our kids for the future, we can no longer ignore this important concept of the light within. It's time to start honoring the light inside our children. And the only way to really do that is by first honoring our own internal light.

How do you honor the light within? Do you take the time to recognize, realize, and respond in your life? Are you aware of your very own magnificence, or do you dim your light because of the cracks in your foundation? It doesn't matter if your childhood was picture perfect or horrific. It won't make a difference if you live in the Hollywood Hills or on the streets of New York City. The only thing that truly matters is that you realize you're an extension of Spirit. To be your absolute best self, all you need to do is connect with that inner light. You can do this by welcoming the 7 Essentials into your daily life. These not only create strong foundations for children, but as you've learned, they can be used to repair and strengthen already established foundations, too.

I know that you may have picked up this book because you work with children, have children of your own, or want to make a difference for children. But in the next chapter, I will offer you the opportunity to connect with that child you know best . . . the child within. We carry negative core beliefs in our hearts because we weren't taught alternatives or shown how to respond to life. Instead, we were taught to react to it. As I've explained, whether we choose to acknowledge it or not, our childhood has an impact on our adult lives because that's where our roots are.

I learned long ago that I couldn't be an amazing teacher or incredible mother if I couldn't look within. One of the first tools I always call upon to help create strong foundations for children is taking a proactive approach with them. If we sit in the seat of judgment with our children, we'll never see their true beauty, nor will we inspire them to shine as brightly as they're meant to. I am a better mother, teacher, wife, friend, coach, and person when I'm mindful and willing to look in the mirror. I guarantee you will be too.

I have a framed picture in my son's room that I'm sure many of you have seen somewhere along the way. It's a picture of a tiny little kitten looking into a large mirror. What he sees reflected back is a powerful lion. The caption reads, "What matters most is how you see yourself." (If you haven't seen this picture, Google it because it's truly empowering.) I encourage you to look in the MIRROR until you, too, see yourself as a powerful lion or lioness.

The next chapter is dedicated solely to repairing and strengthening adult foundations. If you allow the words on these pages to penetrate your mind, immerse yourself in the lessons, and are willing to look within, then you just might experience the light within and reveal your true self. When you're at your very best, your inner light is beaming. It is then and only then that you can help guide our children to ignite the light within themselves.

CHAPTER 12

HEALING THE CHILD WITHIN

"This moment is sacred. I am now ready,
willing, and able to embrace my inner child."

— LOUISE HAY

Linda was a sweet lady with tons of what I like to call "fairy energy"—meaning that she's simply light and airy. She had a huge smile and was wide-eyed and excited by the simplest aspects of life. Linda was always ready and willing to help others. She was the type of person who would jump in and help anyone who needed her, yet she was hesitant to help herself. When she first came to me for coaching, she told me that she struggled with depression. The reason, she said, was because she had studied to be a teacher but was unable to find a teaching job and was very frustrated. I smiled at her observation, knowing that even though finding the position was her focus at the moment, there was clearly much more to her feelings. We needed to get to the major core belief that was holding her back in all areas of her life. We met a few times to create a plan of action for her, and it was clear by the second session that she didn't trust herself to make choices and therefore depended on others to tell her what to do.

Linda had been living with a man for several years while raising her teen-aged daughter, but this man had no intention of making a formal commitment. She told me that she knew she wasn't in love with him but felt that she needed him because he was helping her to support her daughter and provided a roof over their heads. I asked her how *she* felt about that.

She turned to me with tears in her eyes and said, "Awful. I hate it. He's a good person but he does things that are horrible, and he doesn't treat me like I really matter to him. I just feel awful."

I waited a few minutes as she sobbed and I held her for comfort.

Then, she wiped her tears and said, "I'm so angry!"

I nodded my head in agreement and there was a long pause again. I then looked at her and gently asked, "Who are you mad at?"

She quickly responded, "Him!"

I raised an eyebrow and kept looking into her eyes.

She dropped her face to her hands and cried, "Me. I'm really mad at me."

In the next few sessions I learned that Linda felt abandoned by her own father, and so it wasn't difficult to see why she would choose a man who wasn't emotionally available. She'd blamed herself her whole life for her father's emotional abandonment, married a man who emotionally abandoned her as well, and after bravely leaving him with her young child, she hooked up with another man who was totally unavailable emotionally—all because she believed that she wasn't worthy.

Over the next few months, we worked on helping her to change her beliefs by creating new beliefs about herself in relationships and her ability to feel safe without a man. This was critically important not only for Linda but also for her daughter, who, as a teenager, was also learning how to choose a man—whether her mom realized that or not. Linda's most difficult hurdle was releasing her fears and embracing new thoughts. She understood, however, that she'd allowed fear to drive her for years, and it was time to trust the voice within and be guided by love.

A little fear can be a good motivator, but when fear paralyzes us, keeps us in unhealthy relationships, or forces us to shut down our feelings in order to survive, it's time for a change. This fear comes from the core beliefs that we formed in childhood. And believe it or not, that child is still inside each of us. If you want to shift negative core beliefs in your life and build a stronger foundation for yourself, then you need to heal the child within. That little one is still trying to get their needs met, even though you're now in an adult body.

Linda is just like so many of us. She gave all of her power over to a negative core belief that was established in childhood. As a result, she focused on fear instead of love. Feeling unworthy is one of the top core beliefs that my clients come to me to shift. When we allow fear to take the helm, we inevitably become stuck in one aspect or another of life. When fear overwhelms us and immobilizes us, it's time to heal the wounds of the inner child.

When you feel fearful about something, ask yourself what you're afraid of: are you afraid of being abandoned, afraid you're not good enough, afraid that you're not safe? Then take a moment to nurture and love the child within. When fear comes up, that's your inner child crying out for help. You're fearful that what you saw, experienced, or learned to dread in childhood is happening right now. Instead of allowing the fear to overwhelm you, try loving the child within by giving that child the love, safety, and acceptance it needs but may not have received all those years ago. Know also that when you embrace your inner child, you become more available for your own children. You can do this by applying a few simple practices in your adult life and by using the same strategies (plus a few more that you'll learn in the next chapter) for children.

Under Reconstruction

First things first: you are important, you are worthy, you are good enough, and you have everything that you need to repair and strengthen *your* foundation. Just because you weren't given these tools during childhood doesn't mean it's too late for you. If you haven't taken a look at your own foundation up to this point because you didn't feel worthy or important enough to do so, then please do it now. Your children are depending on it—especially the child within.

Our children are a reflection of us. If we're angry and negative, then our children will act the same way. If we're peaceful and balanced, then our children will also be peaceful and balanced. If you're finding that your child is exhibiting behaviors that you feel uncomfortable with, that embarrass you or worry you, then it's time to take a look at your own foundation. Somewhere along the way you have probably passed these behaviors on to your child without even realizing it. While the actions may not look the same, your fears have likely fed them.

There is no blame. Blaming your parents or blaming yourself will not help in reconstructing your own foundation. Of course, when we take a look at our own foundation and realize that we were not given all of the tools that we needed to feel whole, perfect, and complete within ourselves we may feel angry or resentful. But truthfully, those feelings won't help you to grow and flourish. Instead, they'll hold you back and keep you stuck in the same pattern of dysfunction. Think back to the comparison of our lives to a building in Part I of this book. There is a blueprint. There are materials to shape our structure. The workers are our parents or caregivers, and the foundation is our childhood.

When someone buys a new house, they usually get one of three options: a newly constructed home, one that needs just a few touches and is ready to move into, or a home that needs a complete overhaul or renovation. No matter which one you choose, it still takes vision and hard work to make a house a home. It is the same for your foundation. Whether your foundation needs just a few adjustments or a total overhaul to make it feel right, you are absolutely capable of repairing and strengthening it—if you're willing to put in the work. The permits are ready and the materials are waiting; all you have to do is open your mind and heart to begin the journey. It's much easier to ignite the light in our children when our light is shining brightly. So if you're ready, then tie on your tool belt and let's get to work!

The Toolbox

When I moved into my very first apartment, I remember that after we moved all of the furniture in, my dad handed me my very first toolbox. He looked at me and said: "You're going to need these tools if you're going to be on your own." I looked down and saw one of his old metal toolboxes in his hands. I took it from him and gave him a big hug. I looked through the box carefully and pulled out a few tools. I had no idea what some of the tools were for, but I knew at that very moment that it was time for me to learn how to fix and repair things on my own. That was 20 years ago. I still have that toolbox and I still don't know what some of the tools do, but I am so grateful to have had it on hand when various crises occurred over the years. Some of those tools have been of no use to me, but others have come in handy time and again.

In this section you'll find tools to repair and strengthen your foundation. Some may come in handy and some may not. Keep in mind that these are all part of the toolbox I'm giving to you, so use them as needed. The important thing to remember about tools is that they cannot fix things without your help. If you want to be your absolute best and repair and strengthen your foundation, then you'll need to use the tools. I can't tell you how many self-help books are on my shelf that I've never cracked open or that I've read but never actually done the work. Many of you can likely relate to this. What I know is the books that I did read and then applied to my life in a meaningful way really did help bring about change. I chose to put their tools into practice. We always have a choice. That's the beauty of free will. You're an adult now, and if you want to be your best self, then you need to do the work. Your parents, teachers, and caregivers have already laid your foundation—now it's up to you to fill in the cracks.

Before I give you the tools, however, I'd like to help you to fix up your toolbox. Regard this as prep work, just like priming a wall before painting.

Getting to the Core

If you want to repair and strengthen your foundation, then take a look at your core beliefs. Keep in mind that most of your negative core beliefs can be boiled down to one of two things: *I am not enough* or *I am not worthy*. You may say, for example, "I don't feel safe," but if you look deeper, you'll see that these feelings ultimately come down to a fear of not being good enough, smart enough, or worthy.

Sit down in a quiet place with two different colors of index cards. Choose one color to represent the things that you'd like to manifest and choose another color for those things that are holding you back. Start with the "manifest" cards. On each one, write something that you'd like to create in your life (for example, *I'd like to finish my book on time*). Then take a card of the other color and place it right next to what you'd like to manifest. On this card write what's holding you back (for example, *But I'm a wife, mother, teacher, public speaker, and intuitive life coach, and I have very little time*). Now you have one card in the left column on the table in front of you that states something you'd like to manifest and another card to the right of that with a "But . . ." statement indicating what's holding you back.

Do this same exercise with three to five cards of each color. Look at the column of what's holding you back and see if you can find a pattern. Most likely you will. The pattern will help you uncover the core belief that's actually at work. If you have difficulty doing this on your own, then ask a friend or partner to read your cards and discuss what's holding you back. Sometimes other people can identify the core belief before we can, because we're attached to it and unfortunately protecting it.

Next, flip the second column of cards over so that the negative statements are no longer visible. On the backs of those cards, write an affirmation that's in line with what you want to manifest (for example, *My book is completed on time and in the publisher's hands before expected*). This exercise will help you to uncover the core beliefs that are holding you back and will help you to turn your self-limiting thoughts around. Once you're able to see the idea that's been keeping you from success, you'll also begin to notice how it affects you in many other areas of your life, including your career and relationships.

Get Naked and Own Your Power

Be willing to take a long, hard look at your life, your family, and most important, your childhood in a nonjudgmental way. Force yourself to step out of your body (metaphorically of course!) and look at your life as though it's a movie playing on a screen in front of you. Many of us give our power away by looking to others for validation. We tell our story over and over again and ask others for the answers to our problems. If you really want to heal and be your absolute best, then you must get completely naked and be honest with yourself about your experiences. That means searching your own heart and feeling *your* feelings. Look in the MIRROR and see the beauty as well as the darkness, knowing that you're ready to own your power and make critical changes to be your best self.

Walk in Someone Else's Shoes

When a client works with me to uncover their negative core beliefs, there's often a great deal of anger that comes up around the individual's parents or caregivers. This anger is something that needs to be released if the person is truly going to heal the child within. Otherwise, what tends to happen is the same patterns get repeated time and again—no matter how much the person is trying to avoid them. Before you judge the people who created your foundation, try putting yourself in *their* shoes. This doesn't mean you're pardoning them or justifying their choices or decisions, but it does allow you to heal and release the anger you feel inside. While anger holds you back, forgiveness sets you free.

Applying the 7 Essentials to Your Life

In order to repair and strengthen your foundation, you must develop a new practice for yourself. You must love yourself, feel your feelings, quiet the mind, tune in, remove toxic thoughts, speak your truth, and plug in to your higher power by connecting to the light within. We all have daily practices, but we don't always realize it. Consistency is the key. You've lived your life and developed habits over many years, so be gentle with yourself as you add tools to your toolbox of life. You are capable of changing the negative core beliefs that have caused havoc for you all of these years, and you have the power deep within you to do so— you just need to be open and willing.

Here are some exercises and practices that you can incorporate into your life to start rebuilding your foundation. Most of these exercises are geared specifically for adults. However, you'll find that the tools given here and in the next chapter can be used for both children and adults with minor adjustments.

Love Yourself

You're going to start giving yourself all of the love you deserve yet may not presently have in your life. You'll speak kindly to yourself, praise yourself, encourage yourself, and nurture the child within.

1. Sunrise/sunset: How you start your day is how you'll end your day. Think about children for a moment. We want our children to wake up with a smile and be ready to greet the day. I stand in the hall to greet my students daily with a smile on my face so that they feel welcomed and loved every single day. If you wake in the morning, jump out of bed, and immediately begin going about your regular routine, nothing will change. Instead, you're going to start practicing more mindfulness by setting your intention for the day each morning and feeling grateful as you lie down to sleep each night.

When you open your eyes in the morning—before you even get out of bed—take a moment to breathe in life and set an intention. For example, you might tell yourself, *I have all the time I need today. The day runs smoothly.* Make sure you don't include negative words such as *don't, won't, not,* or *can't.* You don't want your affirmation to sound like this: *I am not going to worry about time today.* When our affirmations are filled with negative words, we're opening the door for what we don't want to sneak in. If I affirm, *I am not going to worry about time today,* then my focus goes to *not worrying* instead of toward what I actually want, which is enough time. To be more effective, set the intention with what you truly desire and say it as if it is already happening: *I have all the time I need today. The day runs smoothly.*

Throughout the day, revisit this intention to affirm that it's true. In the evening show gratitude to the Universe for allowing your day to unfold as you intended: *I am thankful for the smooth and productive day I had today.* Even if your day wasn't perfect, find something to be grateful for and focus on that.

2. Mirror work: Each and every day wake up, look in the mirror, and say a positive affirmation to the person staring back at you. A good place to start is simply saying *I love you.* It may feel a little uncomfortable at first, but you will get used to it—I promise. It feels good when someone tells you that you're loved, and this exercise is to help you to feel the love from yourself. As you uncover core beliefs that are holding you back or as you discover goals you'd like to manifest, set your intention for yourself daily and then reaffirm that intention while looking in the mirror. Always speak as if your hope and dream is already happening. For example, you might say, *I am prosperous. I make money easily and effortlessly. I am strong. The Universe is always bringing me what is in my highest good.*

3. Make a commitment: Commit to yourself. Make a pact that you will love the child within by acknowledging your needs and following your new practice. Choose a few items from this section to incorporate into your daily routine and make a vow that you'll continue this practice, just like brushing your teeth, every single day. You wouldn't leave the house without brushing your teeth, so don't go through the day without your new practice of loving yourself.

Feel Your Feelings

Be proactive. Ask yourself throughout the day what's driving you. Are you being motivated by love or fear? If you feel anxious, rushed, worried, or overwhelmed, then you know that fear is in charge and it's time to reach for another tool to rebalance or recharge yourself. Go back to your intention for the day and shift your focus to what you want instead of what you fear.

1. Breathe: Check your breathing throughout the day. If fear is leading the way, your breathing will be shallow, and you may even hold your breath at times. If you find that you're breathing in any of these ways, take a deep, mindful breath. Scientific studies have proven that taking deep breaths in through the nose and releasing slowly out through the mouth calms the nervous system. *Feel* your feelings and breathe through them. Your breath can remind you that you're always supported by the Universe since you don't have to contemplate the process of breathing; instead, it's automatic. Taking a simple breath can bring you back to the present moment when you need it most.

2. Make a feeling wish: When you're experiencing a harsh emotion such as anger, sadness, disappointment, or frustration, take a moment to label it. Fill in the blanks:

Right now I feel _____. It would be nice if I felt_____.

Then take it one step further:

It is okay for me to feel _____ because even though this feeling hurts, I know that all is well and everything is working out in my highest good.

This exercise empowers you to heal the child within by letting them know that it's okay to feel their feelings, no matter how scary or uncomfortable they may be.

3. Fill the tank: Once you've felt your feelings and breathed through them, it's time to raise the vibration by doing something that feels better. Take a short break from whatever you're doing (even five minutes is enough) to listen to music, take a walk in nature, meditate, find humor in something, or write in a journal. Do something that *feels* good in your heart and raises your energetic vibration. You wouldn't drive around in a vehicle with no fuel, because the car wouldn't run. Similarly, think of your emotions as your vehicle and the things that make you feel good as your fuel. When you're low on energy and about to experience a breakdown on the side of the road—stop and fuel up!

Quiet the Mind

It is true that when we quiet the mind, our soul speaks. To be most effective, you must practice this regularly. It's certainly more difficult to quiet the mind when you're already in a state of panic. No matter how busy your life is, it's critical that you take a few breaks throughout the day to just be still and in the moment. If you never quiet the mind, then you'll always work from your head and not from your heart. You will likely feel that your thoughts are cluttered and disconnected, rather than clear and intentional.

1. Take a break: Give yourself permission to take a short break (5–20 minutes) just to breathe. Find a quiet space—go for a walk outside, close your door and turn off the phones, or pull over on the side of the road—and focus only on your breath. Breathe in slowly through your nose and release it just as slowly through your mouth. Focus on nothing but the air that goes in your nose and is exhaled out through your mouth. Imagine the travel path of the air that you're breathing. Listen to the sounds of your breath. Think of nothing else but your breath. This will bring you to the present moment and help you to just relax and rebalance your energy.

2. Go to your happy place: I teach children to meditate by having them go to their "happy place." This can be a real location you've been or somewhere you'd like to go. It could also be an imaginary place. Some people are more visual, so creating a space in their minds helps them to settle into a relaxed state where they can find peace and quiet. Take a few moments to close your eyes, breathe, and imagine white light pouring over you from the top of your head to the soles of your feet. As the light touches your body, feel the warmth like the sun on a hot summer day, relaxing every muscle in your body. Then imagine yourself in your very own happy place, feeling totally relaxed and having all the answers you so desire. Some people like to post a picture of a place that makes them relax in their office or workspace to help them. It's up to you whether you have a physical picture or you take yourself to a happier spot with your imagination. *Happy place* is a simple but powerful tool.

3. Play meditative music: There are many different forms of meditation and several different ways to quiet the mind. If you need soft music to help you to relax, then by all means play it. There's no wrong or right way to quiet the mind. What's most important is that you take a few moments to slow your heart rate and breathe. There are 1,440 minutes in a day. We sleep about 450 of those away, so we have close to 1,000 left. You can take a few breaks and still have plenty of time to live life. If you take a few moments to clear your mind, you'll feel as though you've gained more time in your day because your mind will be clear and your body relaxed.

Tune In

Do you listen to your inner voice? Do you go with what feels right instead of what you think is right or what you're told is right? Tuning in simply means being mindful—feeling your feelings and being in the present moment. It's very difficult to tune in to your own inner voice if you're not quieting the mind. Furthermore, you won't be able to tune in to your children or the children you serve unless you tune in to your inner child first.

1. Trust the voice: When you have a gut feeling about something or you hear a voice within, don't question it—go with it! This inner knowing or intuitive hit probably happens regularly, but you may not be listening. For example, something inside of you tells you to turn down a particular street, but you don't listen. Suddenly you find yourself caught in a major traffic jam. Or perhaps you have a feeling that you should speak up about something, but you stop yourself and stay quiet. Then you regret it for the rest of the day when things don't work out as they should. Trust the voice within. The more you listen, the more you'll realize that your higher self is real and always on point.

2. Find your "mini-me": When you're looking at a child (your child or a child you serve) and you hear the voice within urging you to say or do something, go with it. This instinct is likely your inner child calling out to help both you and the child physically standing in front of you. You have the ability to help your children be their best by tuning in to your own inner child—you just need to trust that.

Remove Toxic Thoughts

While most people's minds are filled with negative thoughts, it doesn't have to be that way. We can all release negative voices and replace them with positive ones by shifting our thinking. Remember to ask yourself several times throughout the day what is driving you. If you're living from fear, then reach for a tool to balance your mind and align with your higher self.

1. Turn the thought around: Negative thoughts are inevitably going to come up throughout your day. When they rush in, breathe and be mindful of your thinking so that it doesn't force you into a downward spiral and shift your whole day. Grab hold of those negative thoughts the moment you become aware of them. First stop them, and then turn them around. Some people like to use symbols for this, like a stop sign. I personally like a little bit of humor, so I have a drawing of an elephant's back end that I use to help my clients stop their thoughts. (You'll find this image in the next chapter.) A few of my clients have told me that when they start to experience a downward spiral into negative thinking, they actually feel dizzy. I encourage them to take their hand and put their thumb to their nose with their fingers tight together to make a line of symmetry down the center of their face. This is a technique to break the feeling of dizziness that I learned in ballet class, and it helps them remember to stop the negative thoughts. Once the thought is stopped, you must turn it around. Keep it simple. Spin the idea around 180 degrees. For example, *I never have enough money* is turned into *I have enough money for everything I need.*

2. 80/20: While studies have shown that 80 percent of our thoughts are negative, that doesn't have to be your truth. After my dad transitioned and I came out of my depression, I decided that life was too short to spend it thinking negative thoughts most of the time. I made a promise to myself that from then on my thoughts would be 80/20—80 percent positive and 20 percent negative. I hold myself to this promise by asking myself when I'm feeling dim if this thought is really worth contributing to my 20 percent. We all need a little time to complain and feel down, but I save that time up for what I feel is truly worthy of my wrath (like fighting for what kids really need from the education system). I found that simply by shifting this ratio around and holding myself accountable, I was thinking way more positively much more of the time. In fact, I was experiencing 90 percent positive thoughts and only about 10 percent negative. It feels really good and life runs much more smoothly when you're able to shift this equation.

Speak Your Truth

When we hold in our thoughts and feelings rather than expressing them, we're only doing ourselves harm. We're dimming our light by not being true to ourselves. You can cause damage to your physical and emotional health by stuffing your feelings and buttoning your lips. When you were a child, you may have been told that you weren't allowed to speak up. But now that you are an adult, you're more than free to speak your truth. And if you do so effectively, you'll empower the child within and feel a whole lot better about yourself.

1. I Statements: I've spoken about "I Statements" quite a bit, and you saw the formula for them in Lizzy's story in Chapter 9. This tool is not something that I came up with. These statements have been used for years in conflict resolution and communication strategy workshops. This is an oldie but goodie.

If you want to get your needs met you have to take the bull by the horns. You can't wait for others to notice that you're sad or disappointed. It would be nice if everyone was totally mindful, but that's not our reality.

Here is the simple formula for this tool:

I feel _____(Tell the person
how you feel: happy, sad, mad, etc.)

When _____(Tell them when
you feel this way.)

Because _____. (Explain why
you think you feel this way.)

What I really need is _____(Share what
you need to feel better.)

Keep in mind that this is a tool you can use to get your thoughts straight before actually speaking to another person. You don't have to use this formula word for word, but it certainly helps take the blame out of the equation and allows you to ask for what you really want. If you share your feelings and the other person doesn't respond in the way that you're hoping for, at least you've spoken your truth and you will be able to move on.

We can't control what other people think or do. We can only control our own thoughts and actions. Therefore, be cautious when forming the last part of this statement that you are not hinging your happiness on what others may say or do. When we wait for others to validate our feelings, we are giving our power away. When we speak our truth and leave it with them—no matter what their response is—we empower ourselves.

2. Imagine yourself at a red light: Many of us react (rather than respond) when people say something that we really don't want to hear. This is probably because their words are tapping a negative core belief. The moment a person taps this nerve and you want to react, imagine a red light. That stoplight is reminding you to wait before speaking. Listen to what the person has to say without being defensive. You can do this by repeating in your head, *This is not personal. This is not personal.* (Even when it appears to be a personal attack, there's usually something deeper that the person isn't acknowledging. It feels directed at you, but it's likely their stuff.) Slowly envision a yellow light as you begin to plan what you would like to say in response. After you've listened and thought about what to say, the light turns green. Now you may go ahead with your I Statement.

You can also use this stoplight technique with children who are reactive or have anger issues. The red light is a reminder for them to stop and wait. The yellow light reminds them to take a deep breath, and the green light tells them it's okay to share their thoughts with an I Statement.

Plug In

You are not alone. You're always supported by the Universe, whether you choose to believe this or not. Remember, you don't tell your lungs to breathe, nor do you tell your heart to beat. Your body functions without your input. The sun rises and sets and the world continues to spin without your help. There's an energy that surrounds us and indwells us. We're all part of this one big, beautiful energy. Source is never far from you and is always available, so go ahead and tap into the energy around you to ignite the light within. Here are a few ways you can plug in;

1. Acknowledge it: Look around. Notice the grass growing, the sun shining, and the seasons changing. Stop for a moment to mindfully breathe in the air that surrounds you. You are a part of this energy that you feel. Embrace and acknowledge that. Notice that it feels good.

2. Tap in: I'm not going to tell you to walk into a church, chant, or pray because that's not my style. It doesn't really matter what you do to plug in to the greater energy that surrounds us. All that matters is that you recognize the energy and tap into it. How do you plug in spiritually? Going to church, practicing a religion, meditating, walking in nature, singing, dancing, playing an instrument, writing or reading something positive are all possibilities. Find something that makes your spirit soar and do it more often. Make a list of these things in a journal and pick one every day. If you make this a daily ritual you won't ignore your connection. Divine energy, Source, Great Spirit, God—whatever you'd like to call it—is always available, but you need to plug in to feel it. When we stop connecting with Spirit, we dim the light within and life becomes more of a struggle.

3. Enjoy ordinary miracles: All too often people think that a miracle is something that's impossible to experience. The truth is there are ordinary miracles that happen every day. I don't know about you, but every time I hear of a baby being born, I'm reminded of the miracle of life. There are other miracles that occur daily that we take for granted. Rainbows are a good example of this. I know that they can be explained scientifically, but there is just something magical about rainbows that takes them into the realm of the extraordinary. Take time to notice the simple miracles in life—the ordinary miracles. What do you find amazing? Learn to appreciate the world around you and marvel at the magnificence that surrounds us. Here are some things that I marvel at: the brilliance of the moon, a beautiful sunset, animal instinct, rainbows, lightning bugs, and a child's laughter. There are ordinary miracles happening every day, right in front of you. Take time to notice them, and you will connect with the light within.

Embracing the Child Within

We show ourselves love by treating ourselves with kindness: speaking kindly, listening to our inner voice, honoring our needs, and speaking our truth. We love ourselves by *feeling* our feelings, quieting our minds, listening to our inner voice, and trusting the Universe and our Divine connection to it. We love ourselves when we *respond* to life instead of reacting to it, when we turn negative thoughts around, and when we plug in to Spirit.

Be proactive. Create a daily practice for yourself so that when life throws you a curveball, you know which tool to reach for. Create the life that you want, need, and desire by shifting your thoughts and experiencing the light within. Make a commitment to yourself that you'll create a new practice of loving yourself and continue that practice. If it feels right, don't stop. Give yourself a chance to experience that magnificent light within by setting your intention and focusing on loving the child deep within your heart. I know that many people think that it's selfish to love yourself, but I've learned it's quite the opposite.

Have you ever paid attention while the flight attendant goes through emergency procedures as a flight is departing? When they talk about the oxygen mask coming down they always say, "Secure the mask on your face before helping others." I traveled with my son when he was about five months old and at the time they said, "Place the mask on your face before you secure a mask on a child you're traveling with." I remember thinking that this was awful because I always put my child first. As life unfolded in the next few years and I encountered many experiences with my son, I began to realize the logic of this statement. If you can't breathe, how will you be able to help your child? If you're not well cared for, you won't be any good at caring for your children. This is why it's critically important to take care of ourselves first. This doesn't mean neglecting our children or other family members, but it does mean putting the mask on ourselves first, so we've got the strength and ability to be there for loved ones when it *is* necessary.

Lighten up! Laugh, skip, and hop! Enjoy life. When I think of kids and why they're drawn to me, it has nothing to do with Vicki Savini, the adult. Instead, it has everything to do with the little kid inside of me. I'm pretty close to that little girl deep within. I have learned to love her like I love no other child. And if you want to be the best for your children and bring out the best in the children around you, then you'd better be ready to get to know the little kid inside of you, too. As adults we take life so seriously. We're constantly focused on fear and hardly ever centered in love. We spend our time racing on that hamster wheel instead of living in the moment and enjoying the time that we have here on Earth with our family and friends. And for what reason? To buy a big house? To drive nice cars? To feel successful in our career? I think this statement, attributed to Oscar Wilde, says it best: "Life is too important to be taken seriously." Don't you agree? Laugh a little. Get in touch with that little kid inside of you and let yourself just have some fun. When you allow yourself to let go and find humor in life everything goes much easier.

When we are upset, frustrated, angry, or depressed we may blame or lash out at others. But we're usually distraught because we have given our power away in some way, shape, or form. When those dark feelings come up, that's the perfect opportunity to love the little kid within by giving our young selves the messages we never heard. Fear comes up because the child within is scared and feels insecure. The old tapes begin to play, and we start to shut down or validate the attached negative core belief.

Instead of allowing the fear to take over, simply breathe. Take a moment to close your eyes and ask where this is coming from. Then tell your inner child that they're safe, loved, and totally supported. Give them what they never had before, the opposite of what they are accustomed to hearing: *you are good enough, you are smart enough,* and *you are worthy.* Embrace that inner child by giving them the security that they needed years ago. Not only will you feel empowered, but the children in your life will be drawn to that light and reflect its beauty. If you truly want to create the best foundation for your children or the children you serve, then you must embrace the child within. Now, go ahead and give that kid a hug—you deserve it!

CHAPTER 13

CREATING STRONG FOUNDATIONS FOR OUR CHILDREN

*"For in every adult there dwells the child that was,
and in every child there lies the adult that will be."*

— JOHN CONNOLLY

As I stated in the beginning of this book, what happens in childhood doesn't stay in childhood. Our early years are truly our foundation in this life, and if we want our children to grow into happy, healthy adults then we need to start by mindfully constructing their toolbox during childhood.

Every one of us has an imaginary toolbox that we unconsciously carry with us. It's what we clutch when we're in a state of panic. Unfortunately, most of us weren't given our tools mindfully, so although they may work for a while, they don't necessarily help us to feel whole, perfect, and complete within ourselves. Some children whine and throw tantrums to get their needs met. That's one tool that they pull out of their toolbox to use when they're feeling fear. It's not necessarily the best option, as it leads to other issues in life for them but nonetheless it *is* a tool. Some children act out to get attention. Their energy may become overwhelming, annoying, or rambunctious. Again, not a great tool, but it serves them in some way. Other children try to act like someone or something else because they fear that they aren't good enough just as they are. They find that this tool leaves them feeling unsatisfied and yearning for more validation. These are all tools that our children create to soothe the pain, and if something works for them, they'll continue to use these tools even into adulthood.

Think about that for a moment. Do you know an adult who uses these same strategies to get attention or get their needs met? You just may. I certainly do. Instead of judging their immature behavior, perhaps the next time you'll be able to look at them and see the child within still struggling to get their needs met and feel whole, perfect, and complete just as they are.

If I need to change the batteries in an object and I have to remove a small screw to get to the battery compartment, I can use many different tools to pry the back off but I may damage or ruin the object. On the other hand, if I take a moment to look at which tool will work best, then I'll remove that screw without causing damage. It's all about choosing the tools that work best and leave the least amount of damage. Having more tools to handle life provides us with an opportunity to meet our needs in the best possible way.

This chapter will give you practices and tools for kids to ignite the light within and empower them to be their absolute best. These new tools will help to teach children how to respond to life instead of reacting to it. The examples I've given in the last few paragraphs are tools that we reach for when we're reacting. We haven't taken the time to survey the situation by becoming aware of the true issue, and we certainly aren't willing to look at alternatives. We're trying to ease the pain as soon as possible and manipulate situations so that we can just get beyond the disappointment. Children and adults reach for these tools when they haven't been taught the alternatives.

This chapter will give you some tools and practices to create a strong foundation for your children so that when they're stressed out, sad, angry, or disappointed, instead of reaching for an unhealthy *reactive* tool—which will only deepen negative core beliefs—they will immediately reach for a tool that helps them to respond to life by learning a lesson and moving through the fear. If we give our children these tools mindfully today, then navigating life's waters will be much easier in the future.

Enter My World

If you were to walk into my classroom today, you'd hear soft music playing in the background and a warm chatter of happy students. You'd smell a slight hint of aromatherapy in the air and feel a positive energy flowing throughout the space. If you took a look around, you might notice that the room is composed of all of the kids' creations and very few teacher-generated materials. You would see that the classroom doesn't even really belong to me, the teacher. Instead, there's a sign hanging near the door with the name of a city—a city within the classroom that the kids named, and neighborhood signs that the kids created. Let's journey through a typical day. . . .

My students walk through the doors and are greeted with a smile. They pick up their morning work and begin working at their desks. If a rumble of loud voices rises, then the police chief or mayor claps their hands to remind the citizens of a noise ordinance within our city. (We have 100 percent employment in our classroom. The mayor, deputy mayor, and police chief campaign for their positions and are elected democratically by the citizens. The remaining jobs are chosen by each student. We all do our best to keep our community running smoothly.) The morning helpers then set up our Morning Meeting and the students are invited to the Meeting Place. Sounds like any typical classroom of a good teacher, right? Well, here's where it gets really good.

When the kids come over to Morning Meeting, they run the regular routine of calendar, agenda, and weather, but then they greet the day with a *positive affirmation* (as I described earlier). That's right, I said affirmation. We start our day—each and every day—with a positive affirmation. As you've learned, affirmations are thoughts that we affirm. They can be positive or negative thoughts. However, I like to start each day with a positive thought and end each day that way as well (you can review more about this in Chapter 8). Next, we go through the regular curriculum stuff. You know—reading, writing, and arithmetic. I could really go through my whole day, but I don't want to bore you. Instead, I want to share with you what's *different* about my classroom that teaches the 7 Essentials daily without a whole lot of effort.

When my kids come back from lunch and they're all jazzed up—as any parent or teacher knows all too well—I don't shut off the lights and ask them to put their heads down. Nor do I expect them to get right to work. Instead, I send them to the yoga circle. I know that the word *yoga* can be taboo in a public school classroom, but if it's okay to use that word with the parents, I go with it. If not, I change the lingo and limit using yoga words like *Namaste*, but we still do stretches. Some days we do yoga and other days we have so much energy after recess that we really need to quiet our minds. Do you know what we do on those days? We meditate!

Ouch! Did she really say that? She must not work in a public school.

Oh yes I did, and of course I work in a public school! At this point in the book, I'm sure you're not surprised to learn that I absolutely teach my students meditation because I feel strongly that this is a critical component to empowering them to be their absolute best. I may not call it meditation—again depending on the composition of the group—but we certainly do quiet our minds as often as necessary, and the kids love it!

It gets better. When my kids have an issue with someone or something, they go to the Mayor and ask for a Community Meeting. This gathering happens in the Meeting Place (which is a rug area in a central location of my room), and all of the children sit in a circle to talk about their feelings. Go figure! They're only allowed to share what they saw with their own eyes and heard with their own ears, and they have to say it in an I Statement. As you know, I teach first graders, and as you've learned from the stories I've shared in earlier chapters, first graders can do the same I Statements that you read about for adults in the last chapter! When a child feels sad, they can choose to write out an I Statement and put it on my desk to talk about with me later or hold "Chakra Bear" (a stuffed animal I'll talk about more later in this chapter) until I come over to see if they need to talk or just want to hold the bear for comfort.

You see, the bottom line in my classroom is that the kids are the most important people in the room and teaching them to be proactive, problem solve, believe in themselves, and speak their truth is number one on my agenda! I close each day back at the Meeting Place. We may sing songs, share our feelings about the day, review our daily affirmation, tell stories, meditate again, do some energy work, or just read together. But we meet once more so that I know my kids started their day in a happy, loving, nurturing environment and they end their day with me the same way. I create a safe setting for them to grow and learn in—not only academically, but also socially and emotionally.

I create this atmosphere because I believe that before you can educate a child's mind, you must first touch their heart. I can honestly say that bullying is not something I see in my classroom—at least not after the first month of school when my kids have experienced what it's like to be in Mrs. Savini's room. My kids learn how to be independent and interdependent at the same time. They learn how to love others for who they are, and above all, how to love themselves. My students feel cared for, safe, and totally accepted for who they are. Don't you wish you had a learning experience like this when you were little? I sure do. That's why I hope to empower other educators to step out of the box and create this same environment across the globe. This is exactly what our children need and want, and there's no reason to deprive them of it any longer.

In this next section, I'll give you practices that I do in my classroom, in my programs for children, and with my own child. Please note that you can adapt anything used in the classroom for your own home as well.

Step 1: Create a Nurturing and Loving Environment

Children can sense the energy in the room or in their immediate environments. If you've got clutter or noise in your mind and you're a teacher, clear it before you walk into that classroom. I have a no nonsense policy on this (ask any of my previous student teachers). I know that you're going to have ups and downs like anyone else but it's critically important that you're mindful when you're with the children because you are leaving an impression on these kids for a lifetime and they don't really care or understand that Ms. Smith is miserable because her boyfriend dumped her last night. As a teacher you need to feel your feelings, but it's unacceptable for your feelings to harm those children.

If you're not in a good place emotionally, then take a day or two to sort it out by looking into the MIRROR and following the *7 Essentials* for yourself. I've had my ups and downs as well and what I've learned from this is that you only have those children in your presence for a mere 180 days, but you'll leave a lasting impression on them and could possibly be creating a negative core belief without even knowing it. Do yourself and the children a favor—take care of you so that you can be your best for those kids. They need and deserve that from you.

If you're not a teacher but are reading this book for your own children, keep in mind that childhood is a short period of time. Of course you are going to experience worry, fear, anger, and possibly depression. I don't want you to shield your children from your true feelings because that's the exact opposite of what I've taught this far about emotions. Instead, I ask you to feel your feelings, be honest with your children when you're feeling dim, and take care of yourself so that you aren't stuck in a negative-feeling place for a long period of time.

Remember that your children learn from you 24/7, so take those opportunities to show them how to handle their feelings in a healthy way. It's important for our children to see us experiencing our own emotions, but it's irresponsible to take out our misery on them. Unfortunately, when we stay in a dark-feeling place for extended periods of time and choose to ignore the alternatives, we end up taking it out on the vulnerable people around us. Like it or not, that would be the children.

In the Classroom

1. Create a classroom community: Think about creating a community within your classroom where the kids name the community, create neighborhoods, elect officials, choose jobs that they're paid for (with community money, of course), and problem solve in a community forum (community meetings). I've taught workshops on this for several years because not only does it help teachers with behavior management in the classroom, but it teaches children how to problem solve. If you want to stop micromanaging and start teaching, then it's time to give the children the chance to have ownership within the classroom. The thought of letting go of control might scare the hell out of you, but I've done this from kindergarten through sixth grade in inner city and suburban classrooms, and I tell you it's the best way to create a classroom where you can teach because you're not constantly putting out fires. Children learn how to depend on one another and also how to be independent for themselves with this model. I could honestly write a whole other book on this concept alone, so if you would like some information on how to start this community—especially with young children—feel free to contact me for coaching on this or upcoming workshops at vicki@vickisavini.com.

2. Appeal to their senses:

— **Aromatherapy:** Kids don't want to hear anyone talking at them all day long. Instead, they want to experience life. Have you ever seen a Charlie Brown episode where the kids are in school? When the teacher speaks, all you hear is what the children are hearing: "Wha wha wha wha wha." Appeal to their senses. I use high-grade aromatherapy in my classroom (from Green Organics International and Young Living Oils). You can purchase a number of safe diffusers to use in the classroom that you can plug into the wall. Check with parents for sensitivities, but most often lavender and lemon are a safe bet. I use lavender when my kids need to settle down and lemon to pep them up a bit. During cold season, I've also been known to use eucalyptus and peppermint. Note that my kids hardly miss school because (1) they love coming to my classroom, and (2) we keep colds away with good aromatherapy.

— **Therapeutic music:** There are very few moments in my classroom when there isn't some type of music playing. There's always a soft beat of some kind in the background to help the children to quiet their minds. I worked in an open classroom for many years with only a few walls, and there was always background noise that could be a distraction. By playing soft, calming music throughout the day, I'm able to help my kids to focus better. I like to use music by Steven Halpern. He has a fabulous arrangement specifically designed to accelerate learning. I use this throughout the day in my classroom. You can find his music at www.inner peacemusic.com. I also use special headphones and a CD created to help children with ADHD and ADD specifically during writing time because I've seen it make a huge difference for my kids. And of course, it wouldn't be a typical day in Mrs. Savini's classroom without some dance or disco music. When I see that my kids are getting bored or overwhelmed or just need a break, I put on some dance or disco music and we rock out for five minutes. (If you have an interactive whiteboard, such as a SMART Board, in your room, you can pull up the Just Dance Wii game for them on YouTube.) This was a great find a few years ago. They can't use a remote to interact with the videos as they can with a Wii, but they can still mimic the dance moves. (Of course, it's important to preview each Just Dance song before playing it just in case it could be deemed inappropriate.) Let them get their energy out for a short period of time, and you'll be amazed by what they can do afterward!

— **Cozy corner:** I don't care if you teach kindergarten or sixth grade, there has to be a space in the room where children can go to unwind. Kids like tight, cozy spots because that makes them feel safe. I create a corner in my room that's cozy (which also serves as a great sensory space). You can make this very easily. I throw a beanbag chair or two in the corner and maybe a few other big pillows with a rug. The corner is enclosed enough that there's only one opening, yet I can see what's going on the whole time. Kids love this space to read with a buddy, play a math game, or calm their bodies down.

3. Tone: Set the tone in your classroom. I hardly ever raise my voice. If my children get loud, I simply get quiet and stare at the clock. One child always notices, and they notify the others (or the police chief notices and claps their hands for the kids to quiet down—that's part of the community concept in my room). Your kids need to know that even when they aren't following directions, you still love them just the same. I have said that many times to my students: "I don't like your behavior right now, but I still love you." They generally don't know what to make of it the first time they hear me say it, but then they get to know me and quickly understand that I really do love them!

At Home

Of course you can try any of the classroom ideas in your home. The big picture is that you create a safe, loving environment for your children so they know that home is where their heart is. If there's chaos or stress within your home and you find yourself reacting to life daily, then your children will repeat this pattern.

Our job as parents, teachers, and caregivers is to guide our children to be their absolute best and help them to feel safe and secure even when there's turmoil on the horizon. Again, remember that childhood is a very short time period and our children learn from everything we do and say. I've learned that the hard way a few times!

Step 2: Be Mindfully Proactive

I am certainly not the only person in the world who can see the world through the eyes of a child. I pride myself on this gift because it's so natural to me, but honestly you can all do this because you, too, were a child once upon a time. Being *proactive* means giving the children a foundation to stand on instead of assuming that they already know what you'd like them to know and judging them if they don't. *Mindfully proactive* simply means that you put yourself in their shoes and guide them toward success. Instead of setting up our children for failure, we need to take a step back and imagine what it feels like to be a kid. I sometimes do this by getting to the eye level of my students when I'm prepping my room for a new year. I get on my knees to see what they see. I also do this every day that I work with children, including my own son. When I speak to them about something where they need guidance, I get down to their level so I'm not intimidating to them. If I am intimidating, they're really not listening to what I have to say because they're fearful.

Take the time to feel the energy of your kids, and before you judge them, ask them questions to understand exactly where they're coming from. When children make choices, bad, good, or indifferent, it's important that they make a connection as to why they made those choices, or they'll make decisions based on what others want and learn to seek answers from outside of themselves instead of within.

Always have a plan so that kids know that it's safe to feel their feelings and share their ideas. Several years ago I had a little boy named Michael in my classroom who would plow through other kids unintentionally because he really had no understanding of where his body ended and where the next child's body began. One day his reading teacher came to the door to get him and he thought he was late, so he ran to get his books and then headed for the door. In the process of sprinting through the classroom, he knocked over a little girl. She fell to the ground and began to cry. He turned and looked but attempted to keep going. By this point the reading teacher was waiting in the hall.

I called him by his first name and told him to come back. As he approached me, he saw the little girl in my arms and put his head down. I looked up at him—because I was down on my knees— and said, "Michael, do you see that Kelsey is on the ground?" He nodded his head. I continued, "Do you know how she got on the floor?"

He sadly looked at me and said, "Well, I had to get my books for reading, and I couldn't stop to say I'm sorry."

I looked at him and asked, "Is that really true that you couldn't stop for one second to say that you were sorry and check that she was ok?"

He looked down at her and apologized. Then he looked back at me and said, "I'm sorry Mrs. Savini."

I gently held his hand and told him, "Buddy, we need to slow down in the classroom. I know that you didn't mean to hurt Kelsey, and I understand that you felt rushed. But try to remember that we always have plenty of time because everything happens in perfect timing. No more running in the classroom because when our bodies are out of control, this is what could happen. Do you understand that?"

He nodded, smiled, and walked out of the classroom. From that point forward, he always had his reading books on his desk so that he was ready and waiting for the teacher. This was my way of being mindfully proactive because I knew it was hard for him to control his body when he felt he would be late.

There are several other ways we can be mindfully proactive for our children.

1. Ask questions. Instead of telling children *what* they feel, ask them *how* they feel. Give them the opportunity to tell you what they're thinking instead of assuming that you know.

2. Make accommodations, not excuses. We live in a society where almost every child can have a label placed upon them. Instead of labeling our children, let's just survey the situation and provide what they need to be successful.

I know that my son doesn't like movie theaters. I know this because instead of getting mad at him when he asked to leave a movie within five minutes of us paying and sitting down, I watched and learned. I saw his eyes get big the moment we walked in and the lights went down. I also saw him cover his ears right before he turned around to head out of the theater saying, "This place is freaking me out." Instead of getting angry with him, I asked him questions so that I could understand what was going on for him. The bottom line is that he doesn't like dark places with loud obnoxious noise, and movie theaters fit that bill. Instead of going to indoor theaters, we go to outdoor movies. And when we do go to an indoor movie (very infrequently), he chooses the seat (usually in the very last row) because it makes him feel more in control in an uncomfortable environment.

Make accommodations based on what each child needs. In my classroom, children who struggle with sensory integration are given tools to help them throughout their day so they don't have a meltdown. They usually have a basket with sensory items in it to help them in difficult situations. For example, they might have a "squish" ball or a ball of hard clay to hold when they sit on the carpeted area of the Meeting Place with other students, so they aren't distracting others. There might be an electric toothbrush for orally fixated children who chew on their sleeves or put objects in their mouths. I have a basket ready for kids who need it, and I teach them what to use and when so that they're at their best. Some kids need this type of accommodation; some need breaks throughout the day in an area like the cozy corner. Others may need a hug. Whatever a child needs to be successful, find a way to make it happen. Being proactive can save a great deal of heartache for the kids and yourself.

3. Read their energy. As a teacher I know that you have a hefty curriculum to get through, but I also have learned that the curriculum won't be complete without mindfulness in the classroom. If the children are fidgeting, there's a definite reason. Instead of getting annoyed or angry or saying, "These kids never listen," take a breath and put yourself in their shoes. Become mindful of what's happening in the room. What is the temperature like? What time of year is it? Think about what the weather's doing at the moment, and so on. I understand that you just want to keep going to get through all of the curriculum, but please take note of the children. If they aren't with you, it's because their minds are someplace else and the curriculum doesn't matter at that point. Don't be afraid to take one of those dance breaks or a mindful walk. (This simply means walking quietly and observing your surroundings. No talking is allowed because you are observing. There are more details on this a little later in this chapter.) It will make a world of difference. As a parent, you can do the same thing. Before you judge that child, breathe and read their energy. Put yourself in their shoes and think about what it feels like to be them in that moment. That will most certainly shift your perspective. Mindfulness is the key.

4. Teach them to problem solve. Provide tools for children to be self-sufficient and encourage them to problem solve by modeling that behavior. When an accident occurs, ask them what should be done about it. The more opportunities you give children to solve problems, the more they'll believe in their ability to do so. You're literally teaching them to trust themselves by giving them the opportunity to make decisions on their own and asking their opinion when solving problems in the classroom and at home. When issues arise in the classroom, I always ask my kids, "Are you being a problem solver or a problem creator?" They love to solve problems. It makes them feel important!

Step 3: Apply the 7 Essentials Daily

1. Love Yourself

Remember when we talked about loving ourselves and I described loving yourself as liking yourself a whole bunch? Well, that's where we need to begin with our kids. When children are young, they're learning how to form and maintain friendships. We help them to understand that if you're friends with someone, you speak kindly to them, treat them with respect, and work together to have a peaceful relationship. They need to understand that they must learn to be their own best friend. They have to sometimes put themselves first and treat themselves as they want to be treated.

Here are some general tools to help children to love themselves. However, keep in mind that all of the tools in this section for the remaining 7 Essentials will ultimately teach children how to love themselves.

— **Affirmations:** Start their day—every day—with a positive affirmation. You can purchase affirmation cards and choose randomly, or you can work on your own with them. When my son is having an issue with something, we create an affirmation to say at the beginning of each day and continue throughout the day. The kids can choose the card themselves and place it in a special place for the day or carry it with them in their backpacks.

Bella (from Chapter 2) and her mom do this together every morning and it has proven to be very powerful for both of them. Mom chooses her affirmation, takes it to work, and puts it right in front of her to recite throughout the day. Bella chooses her affirmation, places in her backpack, and looks at it when she travels to day care or school. At the end of the day, they talk about their experiences. Understand that affirmations cannot be done only once a day if you truly want them to be effective.

In my classroom, we choose a morning affirmation, place it on the front whiteboard, and then revisit that affirmation throughout the day—making reference to it as often as possible. For example, if we choose *I am peaceful* from our affirmation deck, I point out different times in the day when I see that the children are peaceful or I refer to peaceful times in our day. The affirmations have more meaning when we make them an experience.

Remember that affirmations are powerful because we're affirming that statement to be true. This is a wonderful way to teach children to love themselves because they're learning to start their day in a positive way and focus on what they want instead of what they do not want.

— **Mirror work:** Encourage your child or students to do mirror work frequently. Every week my students sit in a circle and look into a mirror to give the person staring back at them a compliment. I generally teach them what mirror work is in the beginning of the year, and we discuss how it may feel funny in the beginning but that it becomes easier as they make this a practice. Students are encouraged to praise themselves for *being* instead of doing. For instance, they might say, "I like my eyes," "I am a good friend," or "I am smart." Once in a while I will let them say something such as, "I like that shirt you're wearing today." But I only allow that if they chose the shirt and it's representing who they are in some way. Above all else, encourage children to look in the mirror daily and either say, "I love you," or "I am important."

— **Praise:** Of course I want you to praise your children for what they do and who they are, but more important, I would love for you to teach them to praise themselves. When a child does something nice for another student ask them how they felt about that. Ask them if their light is bright and how it feels. Then have them take notice of that and praise themselves to you, for example, "I helped Brian when he fell. That means I am compassionate." My kids love coming up to me to tell me all of the good that they do and praising themselves because they know it's important to me. If we teach them to feel proud of themselves now, it won't be difficult in the future.

— **Power Yoga:** I use yoga poses to empower my students. Having the kids say an affirmation while they're posing means that it makes a lasting impression on them. This is what I like to call "Power Yoga." Here are a few Power Yoga poses to try with the kids:

- *Mountain pose*: Children stand in mountain pose (feet shoulder width apart, arms at their sides, shoulders back and head looking straight ahead) and affirm, "I am a mountain. I am strong. Nothing and no one can knock me down." We have our children do this in our empowerment programs, and it has helped them when they feel that they're being bullied or left out. I like to have my kids close their eyes and stand firm. I then walk around the room and gently push on one of their shoulders. Their goal is to stand firm and show me that they're a mountain and they truly believe in themselves. Children remember this when they're vulnerable. I know this because I've had several tell me this is why they love mountain pose!

- *Airplane pose*: Children bring one knee up and gently kick that leg forward and then back. As they push their leg back, their arms outstretch to the sides for balance like they're an airplane. Once balanced with one leg in the air and arms outstretched, the children then affirm, "I am balanced. I go with the flow of life. I ride the wave and all is well."

- *Tree pose*: Children stand on one leg while the other leg bends in the shape of a number four. That foot rests on the knee of the leg that is straight (although they can place their foot on the other ankle if needed). Hands are in prayer position or above the head in a V shape for balance. Children affirm, "I am always growing and always changing. I am peaceful."

2. Feel Your Feelings

Encourage children to feel their feelings by not shutting them down when they're expressing themselves. I know that you cannot possibly listen to every story from every child because there is simply not enough time in a day, but there are other ways to help them express their feelings and learn how to nurture themselves. What's most important is that they feel safe expressing their emotions so that they don't stuff their feelings and create havoc down the road for themselves or others.

— **Chakra Bear:** In my classroom I have a stuffed bear named "Chakra Bear." She sits upon a shelf, waiting to help children who are feeling sad, lonely, scared, or disappointed. I read a story about her in the beginning of the year and teach the kids that they take her off the shelf for comfort when they're feeling dim. Students generally pick the bear up and bring it to their desks when they feel their internal light isn't bright. I notice and go to them as soon as I can to ask if they'd like to talk about it or not. Sometimes they do want to talk about it with the class or just me. Other times they just want to hold the bear for comfort. If you want a Chakra Bear, you can order one from my friend Kia at www.rainbowheart .net. Otherwise, you can use any bear or special stuffed animal. This is very helpful with young children.

— **I Statements:** Encourage children to write an I Statement to get their feelings out and then put it in a designated spot for you. Sometimes just taking the time to write it out or draw a picture is all they need to refocus and get back to their day. I have a template for I Statements on one of my websites that I welcome you to use: www.thelightinsideofme.com/services.

— **"I Feel" Journal:** Teach children to journal their feelings in order to release pain and make some sense of it. Several years ago my student Lizzy (whose story you read in Chapter 9) really needed to journal her thoughts to release the pain. I created the I Feel Journal for my students at that time and have used it annually since. In this journal, children read the original poem that formed my children's book, *The Light Inside of Me,* and go through a series of exercises to determine what dims their inner light and what brightens it. They also write I Statements and affirmations and journal about themselves to gain a deeper understanding of their feelings and learn to trust themselves. To order this journal, please go to www.vickisavini.com/shop.

3. Quiet the Mind

Develop a mindful practice. Teach children how to quiet their minds so they can be proactive problem solvers and respond to life instead of reacting to it.

— **Meditate:** I like to teach my students how to go to their "happy place" (discussed in detail in Chapter 12). They take their yoga mat or towel and either lie on their backs or sit "criss-cross applesauce" for this. I play soft music and gently guide them through a meditation. You can get one of the meditations I made up for my students at www.vickisavini.com/resources.

— **Yoga:** Children need movement. Choose a children's yoga book and do three to five poses a day. The kids don't have to do yoga for a long period of time to reap the benefits. Instead, expose them to it, and you'll see that they love it. Soon they will be coming to you with poses that they made up. Those are always the best!

— **Mindful walk:** Take the children on a mindful walk. I simply tell my students that we are going to take a walk and be mindful. I teach them in the beginning of the year that being mindful means that they are in the moment. They're looking and listening to one person (like the teacher) or they're observing one thing (like the sound of the wind). We walk quietly through the halls or outside. We are not allowed to talk. We're only allowed to observe with our senses. When we come back to the room, they discuss their observations. For a detailed video of how to do a mindful walk, go to www.vickisavini.com/resources.

4. Tune In

Encourage children to listen to the voice within and learn how to trust themselves by honoring the light within. This is where we teach our children to tune in to what *feels* right in their hearts. Teach them the difference between negative self-talk and the loving voice that guides them deep within their hearts.

— *The Light Inside of Me:* I have made this easy for parents and teachers with young children ages 2–12. My children's book is a natural springboard to teach children about the light within. I read this to my students at the very beginning of every year and then throughout the year for reinforcement. Children understand the concept quickly and easily. When their light is dim, they're feeling sad, lonely, disappointed, or angry. When their light is bright, they're feeling happy, excited, proud, or peaceful. You can purchase a copy of the book for your classroom or home at www .vickisavini.com/shop.

— **Guide them to the light:** When children are noticeably distant or anxious or have just gotten themselves into a bit of trouble, immediately talk to them about how it feels inside. Make it clear that when we make choices, we make those choices based upon what *feels* right inside of our own hearts, not according to what others necessarily want us to do. This will teach them to trust themselves more instead of looking for answers outside of themselves.

— **Personal power:** Our personal power is the ability we have to make our own choices—free will. We all have personal power. It's how we use it that makes the difference. Give children the opportunity as often as possible to make decisions on their own. Instead of making decisions for them, give them simple choices so that they'll learn to trust themselves and make their own decisions. This will teach them that they each have their own personal power and are responsible for their actions. They'll learn how to depend on their inner voice to make choices that *feel* right.

— **Fear or love:** Help children to understand the difference between negative self-talk and listening to the voice within. Remind them to honor what feels right. If they get a thought and it doesn't feel right, then it's not the right thing to do. However, if they get a thought and it feels right in their hearts, they move forward with it. For example, when a little boy was sad at one of our camps this summer, my son hesitated for a moment and then went next to him and put his hand on his back to gently let him know that he was there for him. When Nico took action, other children quickly followed. I asked him later what made him do that and he said, "I saw that he was sad and I thought I should go to him, but I waited a second because I was afraid of interrupting the teacher." I then asked, "What made you decide so quickly to go to him then?" Nico looked at me and smiled. "Because it felt right, Mom. I knew it was the right thing to do because my heart was telling me to!"

The easiest way to determine the difference between negative self-talk (fear) and the light within (love) is by how it feels when the thought comes to mind. Generally speaking, if the voice within conjures fear or makes the child feel sad, anxious, or angry, then it's safe to say that's the voice of fear speaking (negative self talk). If the child feels comfortable, loved, or inspired when a thought comes up, then that is the light within guiding them.

5. Remove Toxic Thoughts

Children can be just as negative in their thinking as adults—they unfortunately learn this from us all. Helping them to understand the importance of their thoughts is a critical component to guiding them to ignite the light within.

— **Turnarounds:** The moment a child verbalizes a negative thought I stop them and say, "That's a terrible affirmation. Does that feel good when you think that thought?" We then take a look at the thought and turn it around. I use this symbol to help remind them to turn negative thoughts around.

Here are a couple of examples:

1. **Negative thought:** I don't have any friends.
   Turnaround: I have some friends, and I am learning how to make more friends.

2. **Negative thought:** I'm not good at math.
   Turnaround: I'm getting better at math every day.

Remember: when we think a thought over and over again, it becomes a belief.

— **Thought stopping:** Sometimes it's difficult to stop a negative thought and turn it around with a positive affirmation. When a child is stuck on a negative thought (or when you are stuck on a negative thought), I encourage them to stop the thought by breaking the pattern of thinking. A picture of a bright red stop sign is a good visual for thought stopping. However, I like this one instead and use it frequently for both children and adults.

Yes, it's the picture of an elephant's backside that I described in Chapter 12. I love using this because it usually makes the child or adult smile and it really does stop the thought long enough to go ahead with a turnaround.

— **Is it true?** As I mentioned earlier, I love using the work of Byron Katie, and she has made it easy for parents and teachers by creating her adorable children's book, *Tiger-Tiger, Is It True?* Her work focuses on turning negative thoughts around by asking four questions: (1) Is it true? (2) Can you absolutely know that it's true? (3) How do you react when you believe that thought? (4) Who would you be without the thought? You can learn more about Byron Katie's method at www.thework.com. I was teaching turnarounds for years with kids and just fell in love with her book when it was published in 2009.

6. Speak Your Truth

We've come this far and we can't stop now. Our children love themselves, feel their feelings, and know how to quiet their minds so that they can tune in. They have the ability to remove toxic thoughts and now we must teach them to speak their truth even when they are nervous as hell (this goes for you too).

I Statements are ultimately the same for children and adults. The only difference is that most people think that only adults can use them. I, on the other hand, have found that children can rip these off like nobody's business and feel empowered by communicating so effectively. If a child is upset about something but doesn't communicate their need, then they have little chance of resolution. I believe in teaching children to be problem solvers, and in order to get their needs met, they need to learn to speak their truth. A child who speaks their truth is not a child to be bullied or dimmed in any way, shape, or form.

Here's the formula (the same as presented in Chapter 12):

> *I feel* _____(Tell the person how you feel: happy, sad, mad, etc.)
>
> *When* _____(Tell them when you feel this way.)
>
> *Because* _____. (Explain why you think you feel this way.)
>
> *What I really need is* _____(Share what you need to feel better.)

For example, *I feel sad when you ignore me because we are friends. What I really need is for you to stop ignoring me when I talk to you.*

Now, this is an attempt for the child to get a need met. If the person they're talking to doesn't really care how they feel, then what they think they need might not happen. At that point, you teach the children to come up with a solution so they no longer feel sad. Imagine I said the above statement and my friend didn't care. My new statement might look like this: *I feel sad when she ignores me because I thought we were friends. What I really need is to be with friends who don't ignore me or treat me like I am invisible.*

This will help children to speak up about their feelings and attempt to get their needs met, but ultimately you're teaching them that no other person can totally meet their needs. Instead, they have to find a way to meet their own needs instead of depending on others to do so.

7. Plug In

If you think back to my story in Chapter 10 about the plug hanging out of the wall, you may remember that this symbol showed me that I was totally disconnected. I was the one turning my back on God and disconnecting from everyone and everything. When we disconnect, we dim the light within, which is why I was having such a difficult time releasing the pain of losing my dad.

We can sometimes become cold and callous and often act out of fear instead of love. When I heard the first newscast regarding the shooting at the elementary school in Newtown, Connecticut, in December 2012, my first thought was, *That boy is totally disconnected.* The perpetrator didn't have a link to the real world. He unfortunately did not respect life, and he certainly was not aware of the light within that connects us all.

One of the greatest gifts we can give our children is the knowledge and understanding that we're all connected in our hearts and minds. We live in a disconnected society that breeds violence daily because people don't see the connection that runs through each and every one of us. If we can teach our children to see the thread that runs through all of us and remind them that we're all a part of something much bigger, I firmly believe that hate, violence, and fear will dissipate. When we can see our connection with each other and Spirit, then the world becomes a much brighter place.

Believe it or not, I've had young children who actually say, "I hate myself" or "I can't do anything right." This is because they've been given messages early on that they aren't good enough or there's something wrong with them. With all of the labels we give children in our society, it's sometimes difficult for them to see the light within. Help children to see the light within.

— **You're great:** I periodically walk around my room and kneel down at random to make a request: "Tell me something great about you." Sometimes the child is caught off guard, but they inevitably come up with something. It could be a simple statement like "I'm a good builder." It's important to have children recognize something great about themselves so that when they come to challenging tasks they don't feel completely at a loss. Some kids need help with this exercise in the beginning of the year. These are the children that I focus on first in terms of helping them to see their own light.

— **Separate the being from the doing:** When children break the rules or find themselves in a bit of trouble, help them to see that they're still okay. Children need to understand the difference between their behavior and who they are as people. Kids who struggle with focus or have extra energy have a tendency to also have low self-esteem because they feel that nothing they do is right since they're always spoken to about their behavior. Many internalize this and begin to believe that they're bad children or broken in some way. Help them to understand that it's their behavior they need to adjust, but they are completely lovable and amazing. Find the good in them and point it out as often as possible.

— **Mirror work:** This is a great tool to help children to see their inner light as well. Encourage them to praise themselves for who they are instead of what they do. This is powerful because they look into their own eyes and see themselves as an individual they need to honor.

It's also important to see the light in others. If we stand in judgment, we can never truly be a community. Have you ever heard the Sister Sledge song "We Are Family"? I have a tendency to change words from old songs (well, that one's not *too* old) to teach concepts in my classroom. "We Are Family" has a catchy beat and was easy to change to "We're a Community"! I teach my kids from the very beginning that we are all in this together. We work together, play together, and help one another.

When my son or my students have issues with other children, I try to help them to see and feel what the other person is feeling so they can understand a different perspective. Oftentimes our children get angry or upset with one another because they simply have a different point of view. Instead of judging who is right and who is wrong, I ask them to look at each side and see where the disagreement came from. It's important for children and adults to remember that we all have a light within, and when our light is dim it's because we are hurting. I've helped many so-called bullies shift their behavior by helping them to see the light within themselves and others.

— **We are all connected.** Kids feel energy wherever they go. Help children to *feel* their connection to one another.

A few years ago, one of my students was sad because she was moving out of our school district. I asked the kids to make a circle around the child, close their eyes, and send her lots of loving energy. Everyone closed their eyes and really focused on sending loving energy to the child in the center. The little girl smiled and said, "I feel it, Mrs. Savini. I really feel it!"

After that, all of the kids wanted to feel it too. We turned to make a train so that we all faced the same direction and would be able to put our hands on the shoulders of the person in front of us—still remaining in a circle on the floor. I had the kids close their eyes, take deep breaths, and center themselves by going to their happy place. When the kids felt calm, I told them to ask permission to put their hands on the shoulders of the person in front of them. They all did, and I watched magic unfold in front of me.

Not one of those six year olds was giggling or fooling around— they all felt the power of the next person's energy. At the end, we thanked the people around us and shared. I had tears in my eyes as I listened to what the kids had to say: "I saw a green light going through everyone's heart"—I loved this because green is the color of healing; "We were all just in a really big bubble . . . we were totally safe"; and "I felt warmth all over my body, especially my heart." Wow! Truly powerful stuff.

My students now do this energy share regularly, and this prompted me to teach my children Therapeutic Touch. We now annually invite moms in for a Mother's Day Spa where the children do Therapeutic Touch and a hand massage. It's truly a beautiful experience each and every year.

— **It could be worse.** I have a wonderful children's book titled *It Could Have Been Worse,* by A. H. Benjamin. I read this every year (sometimes more than once) to plant the seed that the Universe always supports us. Sometimes bad things happen, but it's important to teach children that good things always come from those bad things. After all, it takes a little rain and a little sun to make a rainbow. Show the kids that they are always supported in this world. Allow them to see the natural ebb and flow of life so that the ups and downs aren't so extreme, and they learn to trust that everything will work out in Divine timing.

— **Listen to the children.** When my son was five, he asked me what God was exactly. I had no idea how to answer that for him because I'd just walked in the door and wasn't anticipating such a huge question. I looked at him and simply said, "I don't really know, Bud. What do you think?"

He took a few minutes as he looked at the sky and pointed to his chin. He then responded, "Oh, I know. It's the energy of the light!"

Well alrighty then, there you have it. When we give our children the opportunity to think for themselves and we open our ears, we're generally pleasantly surprised by their insights!

I don't talk about God in school or share my views of religion, but I don't discourage my students from sharing their thoughts and ideas because most often these statements are coming right from their hearts. When children talk about God, the Universe, how they can talk to animals, or how they just *know* something in their hearts, don't discourage them. Instead, ask them open-ended questions so that they can explore their own thoughts and feelings and learn to trust themselves. This is all part of seeing the light and being the light.

Moving Toward a Better World

Childhood is our foundation. It's a critical time in our lives that should never be taken for granted. I could go on and on with endless exercises for children to incorporate the 7 Essentials, but I hope that you're seeing a clear pattern by this point. What's most important is that we are constantly teaching our children to love themselves on a daily basis while still being mindful of others and understanding that we're all connected deep within our hearts. Connection brings about peace, love, and understanding. Disconnection breeds violence, anger, and destruction.

I don't watch the news or even read much of the newspaper because I find it to be too negative. A few minutes of the news can put me in a bad mood or heighten my senses and bring fear into my energy field. Today's media generally dims my light and makes me feel unbalanced. There are times, though, when we simply can't avoid the media. These are the times when the news is so catastrophic that even I can't ignore the broadcasts—the Columbine school shooting in 1999; 9/11; the movie theater shooting in Aurora, Colorado; the school shooting in Newtown, Connecticut, in 2012; and the list goes on. When these tragic events occur, our hearts break. We all weep for the victims and are filled with anger toward the perpetrators. It's hard not to have reactions like this when mass tragedy occurs. I, too, have reacted that way.

However, when I've had the opportunity to feel my feelings and work through them, I realize that at one point, those perpetrators were victims. When something horrific happens and innocent lives are lost, we ask, "What kind of person would do that?" Well, the kind of person who harms others and shakes society with their anger is a person who has a weak foundation with many cracks and instabilities. It's the child who never felt loved, who felt unworthy, incompetent, abused, or invisible. I look at these people in a different light when I remember that at some point, they too were innocent children. My thoughts then turn to this question: *What could have happened to this innocent child to make them do such terrible things?*

In many cases we'll never know. Sometimes it's a horrific experience in childhood, and other times it's several hairline cracks that led them to completely disconnect. The unfortunate truth in any case is that somewhere along the road of life, they disconnected; and I firmly believe that they disconnected because they didn't have the tools they needed to be their absolute best. This is not to say that all of these tragedies come from cracked foundations, but sadly most do.

Let's face it, cracks in our foundation cause havoc in our lives—some more detrimental than others. Addiction, depression, violence, codependence, martyrdom, and perpetual discontent are all symptoms of structural damage. We all have cracks in our foundations, but the question is this: will we ignore them and pass on the same structural issues to our children, or will we repair and strengthen our foundations and give our children the tools they need to be their absolute best?

The Dalai Lama is reported to have said, "There are only two days in the year that nothing can be done. One is called yesterday and the other is called tomorrow, so today is the right day to love, believe, do, and mostly live." That sounds like good advice to me. Let's take the time to find our true reflection by repairing and strengthening our foundations so that we can create strong foundations for our children.

By giving our children these 7 Essentials at a young age, we are empowering them to believe in themselves, speak their truth, and create a better world. We have nothing to lose and everything to gain. Deep inside each and every one of us is a bright and powerful light. It is the energy that connects us all and reminds us who we truly are. It's time to stop talking about creating a brighter future and instead see the light, be the light, and above all . . . ignite the light!

❀　❀

MY PLEDGE
TO YOU AS A
MINDFUL TEACHER

I pledge to treat your child like my very own while they are in
my presence.
I will love them, guide them and always see the best in them.
When your child is sad—
I will comfort them.
When your child feels lost—
I will help them to find their way.
When your child feels discouraged—
I will encourage them.
When your child goes astray—
I will gently and lovingly guide them back to the path.
When your child feels scared—
I will hold their hand.
When your child falls—
I will pick them up and teach them how to dust themselves off.
When your child feels lonely—
I will remind them that we are ***all*** connected.
I will teach your child to *love themselves and be kind to others*.
I will encourage your child to *feel their feelings*.
I will teach them how to *quiet their minds* and find the voice
within.

I will not judge your child—
I will *tune in to their needs* and focus on how I can help them to be their absolute best.
I will teach your child to *erase negative thoughts* and harmful self-talk.
I will hand your child a microphone and encourage them to *speak their truth.*
I will do my best to stay in the present moment and teach them to cherish that as well.
Above all, I will teach your child to believe in themselves and trust the light within.
This I pledge to you—
But most important . . . to your children!

ACKNOWLEDGMENTS

I'd like to thank my mom and dad for giving me my perfect foundation, hairline cracks and all! You've always been "the wind beneath my wings" and I am truly thankful to have had you for my parents on this earth. I love you and thank you with all of my heart.

I'd like to thank all of the children who have taught me invaluable lessons both in my classroom and throughout the community. I am so thankful and blessed to have all of you in my life. Thank you for shining your beautiful lights and helping me to see my path so clearly.

I'd like to thank Reid Tracy for seeing something special in me and for allowing me the opportunity to bring such a critical message to our planet. I am forever grateful for your support.

I'd like to thank the Hay House editing team for their kind words and patience with a brand spankin' new author. You're all amazing!

I'd like to thank my husband for his patience while writing this book and his support in my quest to ignite the light and empower children and adults to be their best. You never question me. Instead, your response is, "Whatever you need, Hun." Thank you for that. I love you!

Most important: I'd like to thank my son, Nico, for being the bright light that lights the path in front of me. You are wise beyond your years and I am truly thankful that you chose *me* to be your Mom! I love you more . . . xoxoxo

Finally . . . to all the readers: Thank you for caring deeply for children and picking up this book. May you find peace, love, and happiness deep within your hearts, and may you Ignite the Light today, tomorrow, and always.

Lots of love & tons of light,
Vicki

ABOUT THE AUTHOR

Vicki Savini is a mindful teacher who has been motivating children and adults to be their absolute best for over 20 years. She inspires children to speak their truth and believe in themselves, and she helps adults get in touch with their inner child and understand the importance of childhood.

As a public school teacher, Vicki taught mindful principles in her classroom long before it was considered "acceptable." She is also a dynamic and inspiring speaker who empowers all types of individuals through individual consultations, group workshops, and public speaking. She has experience in the field of psychology and education, as well as in the healing arts and overall wellness; and she is a Science of Mind practitioner, a Reiki energy worker, and a talented Intuitive Life Coach. She uses her real-world experiences and eclectic training to educate, enlighten, and empower individuals to believe in themselves and live their truth. For more information on her services, please visit: www.vickisavini.com.

NOTES

NOTES

NOTES

NOTES

We hope you enjoyed this Hay House book. If you'd like
to receive our online catalog featuring additional information
on Hay House books and products, or if you'd like to find out
more about the Hay Foundation, please contact:

Hay House, Inc., P.O. Box 5100, Carlsbad, CA 92018-5100
(760) 431-7695 or (800) 654-5126
(760) 431-6948 (fax) or (800) 650-5115 (fax)
www.hayhouse.com® • www.hayfoundation.org

Published and distributed in Australia by: Hay House Australia Pty. Ltd.,
18/36 Ralph St., Alexandria NSW 2015 • *Phone:* 612-9669-4299
Fax: 612-9669-4144 • www.hayhouse.com.au

Published and distributed in the United Kingdom by: Hay House UK, Ltd.,
Astley House, 33 Notting Hill Gate, London W11 3JQ • *Phone:* 44-20-3675-2450
Fax: 44-20-3675-2451 • www.hayhouse.co.uk

Published and distributed in the Republic of South Africa by: Hay House SA
(Pty), Ltd., P.O. Box 990, Witkoppen 2068 • *Phone/Fax:* 27-11-467-8904
www.hayhouse.co.za

Published in India by: Hay House Publishers India, Muskaan Complex, Plot No.
3, B-2, Vasant Kunj, New Delhi 110 070 • *Phone:* 91-11-4176-1620
Fax: 91-11-4176-1630 • www.hayhouse.co.in

Distributed in Canada by: Raincoast Books, 2440 Viking Way,
Richmond, B.C. V6V 1N2 • *Phone:* 1-800-663-5714 • *Fax:* 1-800-565-3770
www.raincoast.com

Take Your Soul on a Vacation

Visit www.HealYourLife.com® to regroup, recharge,
and reconnect with your own magnificence.
Featuring blogs, mind-body-spirit news, and
life-changing wisdom from Louise Hay and friends.

Visit www.HealYourLife.com today!